"Very timely read as almost everyone I work with in my psychotherapy practice is incredibly stressed, anxious, overwhelmed, and facing inner turmoil. I recommend this easy to digest and yet profound book to help us all move through these challenging times."

**Cynthia Dallow. M.S., APRN, BC., New York**

"*The Peaceful Warrior's Path* combines vast experience, deep thought, and practical techniques. Some books run away with spiritual matters, leaving us standing where we stood in the bookstore. George's human qualities shine through, illuminating a practical, common sense approach."

**Loren M. Fishman, MD,
Columbia University Medical School,
B Philosophy, Oxford**

"George Pitagorsky is a master teacher of mindfulness-based management strategies. George embodies what he dispenses: practical wisdom that produces tangible results. His wisdom and effectiveness are on par with the best. This, in my view, makes his teaching and books alluring."

**Brian Simmons, Educator,
Meditation Teacher**

"*The Peaceful Warrior's Path* offers a generous, practical, and panoramic approach. This groundbreaking system is designed to give every aspect of one's life greater meaning, success, and fulfillment. It is also refreshingly non-sectarian. George Pitagorsky has created a remarkably complete path to make life a healthy and awakened journey, blending ancient wisdom and practices with modern science to quiet the mind and open the heart for optimal wellness."

**John Bush, Filmmaker, *The Yatra Trilogy*,
*Journey Into Buddhism***

"More than a book, *The Peaceful Warrior's Path* is a manual for optimal living and decision-making. It is lovingly offered by George Pitagorsky, who has spent 40 years developing practical applications for mindful living."

**Dr. Michael Katz, Psychologist, Artist, and
Author of the Well-Known *Dream Yoga* Books**

"By far, this user-friendly, engaging, analytical, and fun-to read-book exceeded my expectation. George artfully and skillfully blends age-old philosophy and proven techniques while holding the reader's feet to the ground with practical exercises. I'd recommend this book first and foremost to those who are convinced they have no time to read such a book."

**Dr. Tsahi (Zack) Niv, PT, DPT, MTC, Physical Therapist
and Owner at MSMPT, Adjunct Professor at New York
College of Podiatric Medicine and NYU**

# THE PEACEFUL WARRIOR'S PATH

# THE PEACEFUL WARRIOR'S PATH

Optimal Wellness through Self-Aware Living

**GEORGE PITAGORSKY**

*The Peaceful Warrior's Path: Optimal Wellness through Self-Aware Living*
First Edition Trade Book 2023
Copyright © 2023 by George Pitagorsky

All rights reserved. No part of this publication may be reproduced, stored in a retrieval system, or transmitted in any form by any means—electronic, mechanical, photocopy, recording, or otherwise—except for brief quotations in critical reviews or articles, without the prior permission of the publisher, except as provided by U.S. copyright law.

Disclaimer: This book is intended to provide information and guidance on self-awareness and personal wellness practices. The information contained in this book is not intended to replace medical advice, treatment, or diagnosis from a licensed healthcare professional. The advice provided in this book is based on the author's personal experience and research, and may not be suitable for everyone. Readers are advised to consult with a qualified healthcare provider before making any changes to their practices or lifestyle based on the information provided in this book. The author and publisher disclaim any liability or responsibility for any harm that may arise from following the advice or suggestions in this book. Readers should use their own judgment and discretion when implementing any of the recommendations in this book.

To order additional books:
www.amazon.com
www.self-awareliving.com

For bulk orders, or more information, contact info@self-awareliving.com

Published by Self-Aware Living

ISBN: 978-1-952943-27-0

E-book also available: 978-1-952943-28-7

*For all who wish to live a happier, healthier, and more effective life.*

# TABLE OF CONTENTS

*Acknowledgments* . . . . . . . . . . . . . . . . . . . . . . . . . . . . . . . . . . . xi
How to Use This Book . . . . . . . . . . . . . . . . . . . . . . . . . . . . . . . .1

## Section 1  Foundation . . . . . . . . . . . . . . . . . . . . . . . . . . . . .7

| | | |
|---|---|---|
| Chapter 1 | Introduction and Overview . . . . . . . . . . . . . . . . . .9 |
| Chapter 2 | Solution: Learn to Play . . . . . . . . . . . . . . . . . . . . .13 |
| Chapter 3 | Treating the Causes: Accepting and Letting Go . .17 |
| Chapter 4 | Peaceful Warrior: Patience and Freedom . . . . . . . .21 |
| Chapter 5 | Courage and Trust . . . . . . . . . . . . . . . . . . . . . . . .27 |

## Section 2  Ideals . . . . . . . . . . . . . . . . . . . . . . . . . . . . . . . . .33

| | | |
|---|---|---|
| Chapter 6 | Calm Center . . . . . . . . . . . . . . . . . . . . . . . . . . . .35 |
| Chapter 7 | Motivation: Intentions, Goals, and Plans . . . . . . . .39 |
| Chapter 8 | Performance, Wellness, Dynamic Balance, and Flow . . . . . . . . . . . . . . . . . . . . . . . . . . . . . . . .45 |
| Chapter 9 | Wellness and Contentment . . . . . . . . . . . . . . . . . .51 |
| Chapter 10 | Ready for Anything: Cognitive Readiness . . . . . . .55 |
| Chapter 11 | Skillful Action . . . . . . . . . . . . . . . . . . . . . . . . . . .61 |

## Section 3  Mindset . . . . . . . . . . . . . . . . . . . . . . . . . . . . . .67

| | | |
|---|---|---|
| Chapter 12 | Awareness . . . . . . . . . . . . . . . . . . . . . . . . . . . . . .69 |
| Chapter 13 | Feelings and Perception . . . . . . . . . . . . . . . . . . . .75 |
| Chapter 14 | Love . . . . . . . . . . . . . . . . . . . . . . . . . . . . . . . . . .79 |
| Chapter 15 | Mindfulness . . . . . . . . . . . . . . . . . . . . . . . . . . . .83 |
| Chapter 16 | Intelligence . . . . . . . . . . . . . . . . . . . . . . . . . . . . .89 |
| Chapter 17 | Belief and Doubt . . . . . . . . . . . . . . . . . . . . . . . . .95 |
| Chapter 18 | Mental Models: Process and Systems Thinking . . .101 |

TABLE OF CONTENTS

| Chapter 19 | Mindful of Process .................... 107 |
| Chapter 20 | Wisdom and Spiritual Intelligence—Knowledge beyond Intellect ............. 111 |
| Chapter 21 | Recap: Relax, Observe, Allow, Do, Repeat ..... 117 |

## Section 4  Practices ............................ 123

| Chapter 22 | Method ............................. 127 |
| Chapter 23 | Training the Mind: Meditation ............ 133 |
| Chapter 24 | Exercise: Meditation Practice ............. 139 |
| Chapter 25 | Body Work .......................... 143 |
| Chapter 26 | Exercises: Body and Breath Work .......... 149 |
| Chapter 27 | Working with Sound ................... 155 |
| Chapter 28 | Make the Best of Pain: Open, Act, and Learn to Avoid Suffering ....................... 161 |
| Chapter 29 | Managing Anxiety ..................... 167 |
| Chapter 30 | Enjoying Pleasure ..................... 171 |
| Chapter 31 | Revealing the Mind: Psychedelics and Psychotherapy ..................... 175 |
| Chapter 32 | Devotion ............................ 181 |
| Chapter 33 | Working with Emotions ................. 187 |
| Chapter 34 | Working in Relationships ................ 193 |
| Chapter 35 | Applying Relationship Yoga .............. 199 |
| Chapter 36 | Working at Work—Right Livelihood ........ 205 |
| Chapter 37 | Community—Friends on the Path ......... 209 |
| Chapter 38 | The Bottom Line ...................... 215 |

*Glossary* .................................... 219
*About the Author* ............................. 227

# Acknowledgments

This book is an expression of gratitude for all the teachings I have received over the years from meditation masters, fellow travelers on the path to ultimate wellness, and the many who unbeknownst to themselves have provided learning opportunities.

Thanks to my life partner, Linda, the loving mirror who reflects the things I like about myself and the things I don't.

Thanks to my teachers: Ram Dass and Neem Karoli Baba who taught the essence of loving, serving and remembering and the critical importance of dwelling in the heart; Namkhai Norbu Rimpoche and Tsoknyi Rimpoche of the Tibetan Dzogchen tradition; Chogyam Trungpa Rimpoche, who initiated me into the Vajrayana teachings of Tibetan Buddhism with his crystal clarity and crazy wisdom; Jean Klein and J. Krishnamurti with their direct and unrelenting direction to discover Self. Thanks to Gabriel Halpern who introduced me to Yoga and to the joy of chanting and song as a means for going beyond the intellect.

Thanks to my Dharma brothers and sisters, too numerous to name who are a constant support in my inner work and a joyful company in the journey we are on together. And a special shout out to the memory of dear friend Sruti Ram Palmer.

Thanks also to the wise input from my editorial and design team at Inspira Literary Solutions.

# How to Use This Book

*"The most difficult thing is the decision to act; the rest is merely tenacity . . .
You can act to change and control your life;
and the procedure, the process, is its own reward."*
Amelia Earhart

The point of this book is to give you concepts and techniques to promote wellness and enable you to live happily and effectively, ready to experience anything you encounter in your life with a sense of ease rather than angst.

For most of us, it takes work, intentional applied effort, to stop holding on to the things that get in the way of living as best as possible, i.e., "optimally." The good news is that the work becomes increasingly easier as you do it, until eventually it becomes effortless and self-sustaining.

Increasing numbers of people in our world are experiencing significant stress, often rooted in financial, health, emotional, political, and relationship issues. These lead to anger, anxiety, sadness, jealousy, unresolved conflict, questioning self-worth, poor health, and disappointments, which, in turn, stand in the way of living and performing at our best.

## Interesting Times

We live in *"interesting"* times—interesting because they challenge us with uncertainty and a sense of *not* being in control. Change is occurring quickly, breaking down not only our sense of security but also our sense of reality. We are faced with diseases, war and the fear of war, the rise of AI, political, social, economic, and ecological disruption, and more. Granted, there have been many times of upheaval in history. This time, however, the speed of change seems faster and, of course, the big difference is that it is we and not people from the past who are experiencing it.

Whoever you are, whatever you do, it IS possible to be both fully passionately involved in life and at peace with things as they are. You can still live your best life—active, comfortable with yourself, in touch with an inner sense of contentment and peace, from a *calm center*—ready for anything.

How to live that way is simple, though not necessarily easy. The key components of this lifestyle are: 1) cultivate self-awareness, 2) accept what you cannot change, and 3) let go into effective action.

This book explores that way as a "path," a path to living "ready for anything" by overcoming obstacles to achieving wellness, with its freedom from unnecessary stress and suffering. As you travel this path, you'll find these obstacles are physical and mental habits, beliefs, and models that drive your perceptions and behavior.

Is it unrealistic to say that all it takes is self-awareness, accepting, and letting go to remove the obstacles that stand in your way? Not when you realize that to accept and let go takes intention, work, patient persistence, courage, and skillful effort. You commit to mindfully noticing what is happening within and around you. And, when you realize you are distracted, you return to the noticing.

## A Prescription for Optimal Living

Think of this book as a motivational prescription for living in a way that satisfies personal objectives for health, happiness, and success, and doing it ethically with kindness and compassion.

Don't expect a simple, straight-line, step-by-step process with exact measurements. This is a set of ingredients: mindset,* worldview, intention, practices, and techniques. You combine them to create a lifestyle that supports optimal wellness. Look for these recurring themes that appear throughout the book: mindful awareness, letting go, and acceptance, along with using all experiences as fuel for increased wellness.

The prescription you'll find here treats a core problem: unnecessary self-imposed stress. This is the greatest obstacle to living optimally with sustainable wellness. This book will provide you with cause- and symptom-removal options. You can choose how much you will treat the symptoms and how much you will use them as part of your work to remove the causes.

Removing symptoms helps to ease the pain but the results are temporary; causes are more difficult to remove. It takes time, sometimes years, of courage and patient effort, to change mental and physical habits. But once causes are resolved, the symptoms dissolve.

To obtain the most from this prescription, add the ingredients of your gratitude, generosity, intention, commitment, and effort. The challenge is to:

- Be grateful for being aware of your ability to use your life experience, pleasure, and pain as fuel for personal growth
- State your intention—why you are reading this book. Write it down.
- State your short-term goals—problems or challenges in your life you'd like to address
- Read the book, reflect on, and begin to "digest" the concepts
- Do the exercises
- Take on one informal practice (to be identified later) and work with it for at least 40 days
- Keep a journal to record thoughts, questions, answers, and issues you want to follow up on

## How the Book Is Organized

There are five major sections: Foundation, Ideals, Mindset, Practices, and a Glossary:

1. Foundation—an introduction and overview to define terms and set the stage for the rest of the book
2. Ideals—Optimal living in terms of wellness, flow, dynamic balance, being centered, happy, ready for anything, and acting skillfully
3. Mindset—the mindset, beliefs, and models that influence the way we live
4. Practices—tools and techniques to promote optimal living
5. Glossary—definitions to clarify terms that may not be familiar to many readers. These terms are noted with asterisks throughout the book.

The approach is non-linear. You can read in any order that pleases you. There are cross references from chapter to chapter to enable you to go between overview and detail and to clearly see the interrelationships among them.

If you take on the challenge of self-aware living, accepting, and letting go, you may return to concepts and exercises for reminders and to see if your understanding has changed.

I recommend reading the Foundation section first for a sense of what optimal living means and the ideas that support it. Then decide how to proceed. You might go right to the "Recap" and "Practices" chapters and then come back to the more conceptual "Mindset" section.

Most chapters include exercises. Doing the exercises brings the content into practical use, sometimes by giving you techniques to apply and sometimes by presenting questions you can use to work with personal issues.

I recommend keeping a journal to record insights from exercises and, more importantly, your goals and expectations and how you are addressing them.

The goal for some is transformation and for others incremental improvement; either way, it's up to you to make the changes in your life that dissolve the obstacles standing in the way of wellness.

There is a lot to think about and to do in this book. Don't try to understand and apply it all at once. Take it slow and easy, but not too slow and easy. Let your mind digest the concepts. Start with wise intention and use techniques that fit into your lifestyle.

For me, the place to start was with intensive breath and body work. Others may be more comfortable starting with informal mindfulness practices like breathers, posture awareness, the study of wisdom concepts, or devotional practices.

However you decide to proceed, set your intention to cultivate the ability to drop into your calm center* over and over again, as you discover the path to optimal living.

SECTION 1

# Foundation

*Once you commit to living as best as you can, you are doing it.*
*The path is the goal.*

This section sets the stage for the process of transforming your life into a path to wellness: living as best you can, optimally. If you are already on the way, see how the Foundation chapters align with your thinking and provide another perspective.

CHAPTER 1

# Introduction and Overview

Want to be happier? More meaningfully effective? Free of the plague of obsessive thinking and worry?

Feeling that you can do more and do better?

Are you . . . stuck? Worried? Anxious? Depressed? Hyperactive? Hypercritical? Addicted? Low on energy and self-discipline? Ready to drop out? Too scared to stop? Too stressed to take a moment to relax? Burning or burnt out? Bored? Fed up?

You may be deeply involved in psychotherapy or already on a spiritual path. Conversely, you may find psychology and the word "spiritual" to be turn-offs. It doesn't matter. When it comes to becoming happier and more effective, what matters is your intention, how open-minded you are, and your willingness to work on yourself to change your mind and open your heart.

The process or path is *not* a climb through stages of development to attain enlightenment; it is a way of life. The path is like a rope with strands woven together: the strands are wisdom, effort, concentration, mindfulness, and skillful behavior. One strand by itself is weak. Woven together, the strands create a strong rope. You climb the rope to reach your goal.

## The Problem: Unnecessary Self-imposed Stress

The goal is to resolve the problem of unnecessary self-imposed stress, which is one of the primary causes of sub-optimal living, draining our energy and preventing us from living our best life. The symptoms are anxiety, anger, fatigue, depression, dissatisfaction, compulsions, obsessions, and being reactive as opposed to responsive. These appear in relationships and personal health, at work and everywhere else.

You may think of problems as unpleasant matters to be dealt with and overcome. Try thinking about them another way: as an invitation to investigate something—like puzzles or mysteries. Working to solve a problem can be pleasurable, even if the problem is never solved. If solving the problem isn't pleasurable, then think of it as an opportunity to eliminate the causes of your suffering or dissatisfaction. If you complain and think the problem will resolve itself or last forever, *that's* a problem.

---

*Wanting things to be different than they can be is the main obstacle to optimal living. Everything is changing. What was, was. What is, is. What will be is yet to be known. We are not in control.*

---

To solve the problem of unnecessary self-imposed stress, we need to discover and eliminate its causes. Nothing in our lives spontaneously exists. *Everything is caused by something.*

The food you eat is the result of the coming together of a grower, the weather, packers, shippers, and sellers. Your mood is the result of your upbringing, your thoughts, your ability to change your mind, and the conditions in which you find yourself.

Every problem, every solution, everything, is the result of causes and conditions. Everything is in continuous motion as causes and conditions arise, have their effects, and pass on. To solve the problem of self-imposed stress, find its causes, and do something about them; that something is the "path" or "method." And, it begins with the awareness that there is unnecessary stress.

## INTRODUCTION AND OVERVIEW

*(See the chapters on Intelligence, Mental Models, and Process for more about the workings of the mind that effect behavior and contribute to, moderate, or eliminate stress.)*

Search for "stress" and you will find lists of five, six, and seven causes. The Buddha summed them up as attachment, aversion, and ignorance. They are the primary obstacles to optimal living:

- Attachment—clinging* to what cannot be kept; needing things to be different than they can be
- Aversion—clinging to the need to push away, and deny what you feel is unpleasant
- Ignorance (also called delusion)—*not* knowing and accepting the reality of interdependence, inevitable change, uncertainty, a false sense of self, and that things will not always go as you'd like them to

You can blame your stress on parents, partners, co-workers, fate, karma, or any number of other things, but that will get you nowhere near a solution. Address the three primary causes and you are on your way to wellness.

Of these three major causes of self-imposed stress, ignorance is the root and the most difficult to address, primarily because we are often unaware of our ignorance. Or, we are attached to it, believing that "ignorance is bliss." Wisdom, knowing how things are, is the antidote to this condition. *(See the chapters on Belief and Doubt and Wisdom to explore this concept further.)*

Attachment and aversion drive us to waste energy on trying to achieve the impossible. When we don't get what we want, we are miserable, or at best dissatisfied. When we obtain what we want, we are often disappointed. We might blame ourselves, others, or fate; we become angry and/or depressed. Averse to discomfort, we might never do what is needed to cultivate wisdom.

For example, we suffer unnecessarily when we resist inevitable change or deny uncertainty.

Attachment and aversion can make pleasant experiences painful. How quickly does the pleasure of an ice cream treat turn to suffering when you are unhappy because there is no more, or you start thinking about your weight, or cholesterol?

Attachment and ignorance make unpleasant things worse. Take Jim, for example. He is a performance artist in his late sixties with a bad back and a recent diagnosis of a blood disorder. Jim, attached to his belief that life will be meaningless unless he can perform, denies the reality of his physical condition, and cuts off the possibility of alternatives. Yet, on a deep level he knows he might *not* be able to do what he thinks he *must* do. It freaks him out; he suffers.

Self-awareness leads to wisdom.* Wisdom overcomes ignorance and enables acceptance. Acceptance overcomes attachment and aversion. With acceptance comes letting go into wellness.

## EXERCISE
### Clinging

Over the next few weeks, each time you feel stressed, anxious, angry, depressed, bored, or jealous, ask yourself, "What am I clinging to? What belief am I holding onto that is not in sync with reality?"

Also, note the moments that are light and happy, delighted, mindless, focused, in bliss, or joyful.

Journal your answers and the way the question shifts your thoughts and feelings.

Review the results. Is it true that self-imposed stress is caused by clinging—i.e., attachment and aversion? How does knowing that change the way you think and feel? Does it help you avoid blaming yourself, others, or fate for your reactions? Does just raising the questions relieve the feelings?

CHAPTER 2

# Solution: Learn to Play

*"You have two choices: to control your mind
or to let your mind control you."*
Paulo Coelho

Most problems have solutions. The solution to the problem of self-imposed stress is to change your mind, to break the mental habits that *cause* ignorance, attachment, and aversion.

Neuroscience and common sense agree that the way we think and act can change the way we think and act. This is neuroplasticity: the ability of the nervous system to change, to rewire, in response to stimuli such as exercise, meditation, changed environment, making art, or playing video games.

Changing your mind is a process, a game. And, the first step is to make the decision to play, to find joy in your life. Take it too seriously and you add stress. Let go and you fly. But let go without wisdom and self-discipline and you may never take off or, if you do, you may fall into the sea, like Icarus in the Greek myth.

Once you decide to play, get out of your comfort zone, courageously and patiently. Then you can find yourself truly comfortable, no longer a slave to old habits, biases, and unfounded beliefs. *How can that be,* you might be asking, *How can I get out of my comfort zone and still feel comfortable?* It makes sense if you realize that only by experiencing discomfort can you accept it, find its cause, know you can handle it, and let it be okay.

My Tai Chi teacher says that if you continue to avoid "healthy discomfort," you will not build strength, flexibility, balance, and resilience. Another teacher, Tsoknyi Rinpoche, fears heights. He tells the story of how he would not step out onto a bridge over a deep chasm. The bridge's surface was transparent. Even after seeing his friends cross the bridge without falling, he couldn't go forward. Only by stepping out onto it could he overcome his fear. Once he did, he was comfortable walking across the bridge.

Accept the discomfort of stepping out into new ways of thinking and you can change your mind. Neuroplasticity* is the scientific basis for confidence in our ability to change. If the way we think and act can change the way we think and act, then it pays to be careful of the ways we think and act.

## Beyond Conceptual Thinking

To change the way we think uses conceptual thinking to go beyond conceptual thinking to experience. If this doesn't make sense, you might be thinking that your conceptual mind will solve your problems.

Conceptual thinking is a powerful tool but it is easy to become stuck in a futile attempt to make sense of things that are real and true but make no sense. Become comfortable with both/and thinking, paradox, and *not* knowing in order to experience the *mystery*.

One thing that can enable us to step out of the comfort zone and go beyond conceptual thinking is the ability to step back and objectively observe oneself while being fully engaged. Have you experienced a moment of being in "the Zone,"* in Flow,* performing at your best, and at the same time observing it all without thinking about it?

In that moment, you experience a natural quality of mind that objectively observes without thinking about observing or about what is being observed. This is mindfulness. With it, you can experience everything around as if it were a tragicomic movie, while at the same time being completely engaged. There is experiencing without thinking about the experience.

Jean, a corporate leader who was trained as a gymnast, said that if she started thinking about what she was doing during an event, she was sure to fall. Many pianists describe a similar experience. Without thinking about it, their fingers fly across the keys. If they stop to think about it, they fumble.

Applying this understanding to leadership or any activity is a challenge. This book aims to help you cultivate the tools—mindfulness, worldview models, and other concepts—to use in daily life to increasingly experience Flow, to be responsive rather than reactive in the face of uncertainty and change.

## Creating Your Personal Path

To solve the problem, you'll need to create a path or process for yourself that confronts attachment, aversion, and ignorance with self-awareness, acceptance, and letting go. The path to optimal living combines concepts and methods that will move you forward toward this goal with the courage and perseverance of a peaceful warrior.*

For thousands of years, wisdom traditions have given us the tools and concepts needed to change the mind. Methods and mindsets from these traditions make it possible to be content and effective, even when reacting as if you were the very opposite of content and effective. These tools and concepts are used to consciously change mental habits to promote greater clarity and the wisdom it brings.

As you read on and practice, see for yourself. If something makes you less stressed, happier, and better able to function in the world, and does no harm, do it. If you encounter an obstacle, stop, consider it, and do your best to accept and let it go.

You won't need any extra equipment. The path uses what you have: your emotions, mind, body, breath, work, relationships, and your capacity to be self-aware and self-managing. *(See the sections on "Mindset" and "Practices" for concepts and methods for use in your journey.)*

The path has no finite end. It is an ongoing process. The path IS the goal—sustained wellness living in dynamic balance,* fully involved while calmly experiencing life objectively. It requires actively going with the flow, as a skier rides the mountain or a sailor the wind.

*The process is its own reward.*

To cultivate wellness, a basic principle is to commit to a background task that operates while you are doing whatever else you do in life. It is like the wellness monitor in a smart watch that counts steps and tells you your pulse rate. The task is to use everything in your life as fuel for the journey.

The path starts whenever you are ready to solve the problem. Make the best of whatever comes your way by accepting and letting go, allowing, adjusting, and responding. Rely on the wisdom of the past and question everything, including your own opinions, intuition, and what is preached by pundits, experts, and spiritual teachers.

EXERCISE

## The Solution

Identify ways that staying in your comfort zone keeps you from resolving the long-term issues that cause you to be stressed and less able to operate in your relationships and job.

Commit to playfully extending your comfort zone over several months by taking calculated risks. Be kind and gentle to yourself. Think of how a snake removes its old skin. You damage the snake by tearing the skin off before it is ready. But also, be fierce enough to push the edge, to extend your comfort zone gradually.

CHAPTER 3

# Treating the Causes: Accepting and Letting Go

*"A sum can be put right: but only by going back till you find the error and working it afresh from that point, never by simply going on."*
C.S. Lewis, *The Great Divorce*

To solve problems, address their causes.

This chapter explores more deeply the recurring theme *accept and let go*. Self-imposed stress is the problem that prevents us from living as best we can, content and effective. Accepting and letting go is the solution that cuts off the roots of the causes: attachment, aversion, and ignorance.

## Active Acceptance

There is often misunderstanding about what it means to accept things as they are. Accepting things as they are does *not* imply passively keeping them as they are. For example, you might experience an ache; before you can feel better, you must acknowledge it. Only then are you free to address it.

The Serenity Prayer sums up the wisdom of active acceptance:

*"Grant me the serenity to accept the things I cannot change,
The courage to change the things I can, and
The wisdom to know the difference."*
Reinhold Niebuhr

Whether you are praying to a higher power or talking to your inner self, the Serenity Prayer is a great mantra* to remind you and train the mind to accept and let go. When you are anxious, take a breath, bring your attention to the sensation of your body, and repeat the poem/mantra to yourself. Calm down. Then, with doing nothing as an option, choose what to do. Accept that you can't change the past or the present moment. But while you are *not* in full control, you can act to influence the future, the next moment. Accept, let go, respond, accept, and let go again.

Turn your attention to what you *can* do to make things better. Patiently do what you can, accepting painful experiences, failures, and setbacks so you can grow from them.

Attachment and aversion—clinging to what you like and pushing away what you don't—are habits. If you have ever tried to break a habit or to stop obsessing about something, you know it takes motivation and persistence. But when you do break the habit, you experience calm, confidence, equanimity,* and serenity.*

When you accept things as they are, you are on a solid foundation for skillful response.

## Accept and Let Go

Accepting and letting go are the only logical things to do.

*For, after all, the best thing one can do when it is raining is let it rain."*
Henry Wadsworth Longfellow

Imagine clinging to a branch on the bank of a rushing river for fear of being carried away by the current. There is no way to climb up the riverbank. The choices are to keep clinging or accept your situation and let go to drop into the river.

Why spend so much of your energy holding onto the riverbank, to the known, when you will eventually become worn out and be forced to let go? Choose to let go before you are so exhausted you are too tired to swim.

When you let go, the river takes you downstream. Swimming against the current will tire you out. The river is stronger than you. Let go, stop clinging, and you will find the energy to navigate the river as best you can, avoiding obstacles, riding the rapids, and cutting across the current to reach the other shore.

Optimal living is letting go into life's flow, steering to avoid obstacles and making the best of the situation.

## Surrender to Reality: *Wabi-Sabi*—Perfect Imperfection

Surrender to reality. Things are as they are—impermanent, uncertain, sometimes painful, out of your complete control. So why waste your energy and make yourself miserable? Let go of the need to change what cannot be changed or avoid the unavoidable.

Recognizing and accepting that unpleasant, unwanted *stuff* happens enables letting go. Here is an example of how that attitude is applied in life situations:

> *The great cellist Yo-Yo Ma had a string break in the middle of a performance. Rather than being set off balance by the disturbance, he was practicing* wabi-sabi, *cool and accepting. Equanimous.*\*

*Wabi-sabi* is a philosophy and aesthetic that centers around an appreciation of imperfection, impermanence, and incompleteness.[1]

---

[1] Johnson, Matt, Ph.D., "Wabi-Sabi and the Psychology of Imperfection," *Psychology Today*, July 5, 2022, https://www.psychologytoday.com/us/blog/mind-brain-and-value/202207/wabi-sabi-and-the-psychology-imperfection#_=_

Perfection is an aspiration. Over perfecting—perfectionism—stands in the way of accomplishment just as much as *not* aspiring. The paradox is to work toward perfection while accepting imperfection—*wabi sabi*.

When you accept that "bad" things happen, they become opportunities for personal growth.

*"There's a crack, a crack in everything; that's how the light gets in."*
Leonard Cohen

Thinking it's all perfect just as it is, imperfections included, sets you up for being able to manage your performance most effectively. It motivates you to cultivate adaptability, resilience, and patience.

Imagine how it might have been had Yo-Yo Ma not been so equanimous, calmly accepting the situation. Likely, his performance would have suffered.

### EXERCISE
### Acceptance

Each time you make a mistake, lose your temper, find yourself unable to decide, or experience anxiety or any other difficult emotion, remind yourself that you can accept experiencing it without judging yourself for having it or feeding the need to rid yourself of it.

Accept and go forward, like a figure skater who falls during her Olympic routine, gets up, and continues.

Journal the times you catch yourself and accept. How does it feel when you do it?

CHAPTER 4

# Peaceful Warrior: Patience and Freedom

*"The sacred warrior conquers the world not through violence or aggression but through gentleness, courage, and self-knowledge. The warrior discovers the basic goodness of human life and radiates that goodness out into the world for the peace and sanity of others."*
Chogyam Trungpa Rinpoche

It's simple: become self-aware, accept, let go, and you are free. But it is *not* so easy. This chapter challenges you to work your personal path as a *peaceful warrior* dedicated to personal freedom and expanded self-awareness. A peaceful warrior lives with the intention to improve their own wellness, and to improve the wellness of those around them. (You can use the image of a courageous explorer or an objective scientist, if the imagery of a "warrior" doesn't feel right.)

The image of the peaceful warrior comes from an ancient Tibetan prophecy that tells of how regular people rise to bring about profound change using the powers of compassion and insight. These "warriors" seek an unbiased mind, and to overcome whatever opposes or impedes the way of peace and harmony.

Peaceful warriors work toward perfection while accepting imperfection. They are patient, generous, grateful, and kind to themselves and others, realizing that old habits are hard to break. They treat each slip-up, challenge, disappointment, or failure as a learning opportunity and grow from it. They don't expect to ever achieve perfection but are committed to working toward it. They don't suppress or bypass painful emotions.

They go beyond concept to experience the felt sense* of being present and aware.

> *"Felt sense is the wordless, thought-free, direct experience of what we are feeling. It is related to gut instinct and to proprioception, the ability to sense movement, action, and location. It is what scientists call enteroception, the sense of the internal state of the body that is important for maintaining balance and enabling self-awareness.*
>
> *On a psychological level, felt sense 'lies behind your thoughts and feelings and is significant and full of meaning. It is a message from your body to you and will speak to you when you listen.'"*[2]

Everything becomes fuel for personal growth.

## The Cost of Entry: Patience

The peaceful warrior knows that patience is *not* inaction; it is the base for skillful action.

To be a peaceful warrior you do not have to become a meditator, yogi, or take on any "ism" or "anity." You do not have to lose your ego or drop out. The only prerequisite for overcoming attachment, aversion, and ignorance is patient persistence motivated by being fed up with the self-imposed limitations, the clutter, that gets in your way.

---

[2] Bell, Andrea L., LCSW, SEP, "Felt Sense: The Vitality and Liveliness of Our Inner World," *Good Therapy*, GoodTherapy.org, November 22, 2016, https://www.goodtherapy.org/blog/felt-sense-vitality-liveliness-of-our-inner-world-1122165

## PEACEFUL WARRIOR: PATIENCE AND FREEDOM

Peaceful warriors mindfully observe, use their intelligence, and cultivate a realistic worldview, wise intention, and skillful action. They seek to achieve behavioral goals not limited to earning more money or finding the right partner, car, or home. Their goals include happiness, wellness, effectiveness, being of service, being kind, and finding love.

Patience is a key attribute of a peaceful warrior—the ability to accept or tolerate things you don't like without becoming angry or upset. It is the capacity to be responsive when faced with the unpleasantness of not getting what you want, or of delays, trouble, and suffering.

Patience is an essential quality needed to break the often deeply embedded habit of clinging. It may take decades to fully let go. When we cultivate realistic, rational expectations, we cultivate patience, which is key for developing healthy relationships.

> *"There is nothing pleasant at all about anger. Irritation, agitation, impatience, sullenness, spite—all these sorts of negative emotions overwhelm us and refuse to give us one moment's peace, whereas when we have patience, we have genuine peace. There is no question of which is preferable."*[3]
> Lama Zopa Rinpoche

Recently, I was on a flight from Denver to New York City. The flight was diverted to Harrisburg, Pennsylvania, forcing me to stay overnight. The next day, the flight to NYC was to take off at 11:30 a.m. The crew was on board and ready to go, but the airport agents found it necessary to rebook all the passengers onto the continuing flight because the flight number had changed. This took two hours. Patience was a challenge, but it was a far better choice than letting the annoyance at the weather and the bureaucratic process turn to anger.

---

[3] Rinpoche, L. Z., *Patience: A Guide to Shantideva's Sixth Chapter*, Kindle Android version, 2020, loc 332.

Can you be too patient? Sure, nothing is all good all the time. Skillful patience is not withdrawal and inaction. It is much more intentional than that. It takes patient effort to cultivate patience until it becomes a natural response to discomfort. It is worth the effort. Patient, you are in a better position to respond skillfully and thoughtfully to whatever is challenging you. You experience calm peacefulness, making the best of your situation.

## Freedom

> *"Emancipate yourselves from mental slavery.*
> *None but ourselves can free our minds."*
> Bob Marley

If you are ready to embark on the peaceful warrior's quest for freedom, you'll need to let go of the unfounded beliefs, habits, and mental models that unconsciously drive your behavior. This will free you to overcome the fear of the unknown that keeps you locked into a comfort zone you may not really find that comfortable.

You are free when you courageously accept *reality\** and stop clinging to what you like and pushing away or denying what you don't like. *(For more on what "reality" means, see the chapters on View and Wisdom.)*

Peaceful warriors know how to use their sword and shield skillfully. They attain freedom by feeling emotions deeply, taking the risk of letting down more often the shield they might otherwise use to keep them emotionally safe. The shield is the thoughts and reflections used to suppress or avoid painful emotions. Warriors make sure they use the sword of their speech and actions with kindness* and compassion* for themselves and others.

Philosophy and neuroscience both recognize that the heart (the seat of emotions), the body (the seat of physical sensations), and mind (the seat of cognitive thought) are inseparable. The *heart-mind* represents the combination of heart and mind: emotion and reason, thoughts and feelings.[4] These affect and are affected by the workings of the body as stress levels cause changes in the immune system, heart rate, and other physical functions.

Peaceful warriors risk the pain of opening their heart and shaking the foundation of their belief systems by opening their mind. They patiently cultivate a healthy balance among thoughts, feelings, intellect, and intuition. They tune in to their body and work to keep it healthy.

## Gratitude

I am grateful for being able to serve by sharing my knowledge and experience.

Authentic gratitude is another hallmark of the peaceful warrior, a felt sense, a deep feeling. It is the recognition of blessings (or positive experiences, if "blessings" seems too spiritual for you). It feels wonderful when gratitude is free of guilt or obligation—neither saying thank you because it is socially expected nor feeling that some repayment is necessary.

## Generosity

Peaceful warriors practice generosity, the unselfish giving of something of value without the expectation of anything in return. Perhaps the greatest thing we can give is the work on ourselves that enables us to be good partners, citizens, parents, and coworkers. As peaceful warriors, we cultivate the understanding that it is through giving that we express our compassion and gratitude. We recognize

---

[4] Shun, Kwong Loi. Mencius. In Zalta, Edward N. (ed.). Stanford Encyclopedia of Philosophy and https://www.frontiersin.org/articles/10.3389/fpsyt.2022.802606/full

that giving does not diminish us but gives us a sense of fullness and an opportunity to confront our sense of not having enough.

### EXERCISE
### Overcoming Impatience

When you are waiting—for an appointment, in a line, waiting to be served, stuck in traffic, or waiting for a bus or train—feel the physical sensations of impatience, subtly smile to yourself, and repeat the mantra, "Happily waiting."

Note what happens to your stress level. What does impatience feel like? Does the impatience lessen as you observe it?

Record the experience in your journal. Does repeating the exercise several times over the next weeks make a difference in the intensity and duration of your impatience?

If you are never impatient, be happy with that. Though you might find it interesting to reflect on what makes you patient. Is it fear of what happens if you express impatience or a natural expression of a well-trained mind?

CHAPTER 5

# Courage and Trust

*". . . the game is not to push away the world, the game is not to get caught in it—the game is to, as Christ said, 'Be in the world, but not of the world,' to be simultaneously empty and full, to be somebody and nobody. It's all these paradoxes you have to embrace. There's nothing to do, so get on with it."*
Ram Dass

The Seva Foundation is a non-profit organization dedicated to the serious work of eradicating blindness. I'm told that at its board meetings there was a rule that anyone who said, "Seriously?" would have to wear Groucho Glasses (with nose and mustache attached) for the rest of the meeting.

That being said, the warrior's journey is indeed serious stuff. Overcoming impatience, and other forms of self-imposed stress, affects the way we live. But don't take it so *seriously* that you lose sight of the need to lighten up. Strive to be lighthearted—with a heart full of light. Think of the journey as a game.

Feel fully. Cry when you need to. Laugh a lot. If you become angry or anxious, refrain from letting feelings like that drive your behavior and unduly influence your life. Let yourself be happy.

## From Concept to Experience

Stepping back, you can find freedom by transforming conceptual understanding to experiential *knowing*.

I attended Naropa Institute for a summer program. The program combined intensive conceptual learning about the nature of mind and Buddhist philosophy and psychology with experiential learning through meditation and group processes. There were also some great parties. While I thoroughly enjoyed the crystal clarity of the intellectual part of the program, it was the experiential that had the greatest impact.

---

*Describing the taste of sugar fails to communicate the experience.*

---

No words can fully describe an experience. Explanations and descriptions are food for the intellect. They point to or describe experience. But do not mistake conceptual understanding for the felt sense of experience.

## Paradox: Both/And Thinking

*"Everything should be made as simple as possible, but no simpler."*
Albert Einstein

If complexity, uncertainty, and ambiguity are stressful, it is a sign there is attachment to being in control and knowing definitively. It is a sign you have become too serious. Both/and thinking sets the mind in the right direction for letting go.

The serious work is to learn to take joy in not knowing. There are no either/or answers to complex questions. Paradox—seemingly senseless and illogical statements—can jar the mind to take you beyond rational, linear thinking, from conceptual knowing to experiential knowing.

Overcome the stress of having to figure everything out.

The story of Marpa's grief at the loss of his son brings out the paradox between managing and fully experiencing emotions:

> *Marpa, a great enlightened master in the Tibetan Buddhist tradition, was at the funeral of his son who had died in an accident. Marpa was weeping. A student asked, "Why, if this life is all an illusion, would the master be upset?" Marpa answered that the death of a child is like a nightmare, a super-illusion, more painful than anything. Even though this intense grief was a momentary experience caused by attachment, it was to be fully accepted though not fed so that it becomes depression or anger.*

## Courage

It takes courage to stop taking yourself and your beliefs so seriously and to accept the reality that there are things you will not know with your conceptual mind.

> *Courage does not mean being without fear.*
> *It means being able to experience fear and not be driven by it,*
> *running from it, or turning it into aggression.*

A fireman's training and equipment are useless if he runs away from the smoke, heat, and uncertainty of the fire. The fireman's courage comes from confidence through practice, respect for fear, and acceptance of the possibility of injury and death.

Some are willing to stay with a miserable situation, "the devil they know," to avoid the discomfort of change and uncertainty, even though they know those are unavoidable.

If fear is keeping you from letting go, summon the courage to let go into uncertainty. The fearful person can make anything an excuse for avoiding reality. Even the notions of being enlightened or aware, nirvana, heaven, etc. can be ways to avoid the unknown by creating an illusion of certainty. Therefore, Zen master Lin Chi* said, "If you meet the Buddha, kill him." He meant that anyone who thinks they possess all the answers had better think again. It takes courage to refrain from making any image, hero, saint, faith, or ism into an idol that will protect you.

## Faith or Trust

Courage rests on faith or trust. Firm belief is not blind faith. It is earned through experience, questioning, testing, and validation.

If you have faith that lifting weights, stretching, and running are good for you, you do them. If they work well, you keep doing them. If, on the other hand, you start developing pulled muscles, achy joints, and other effects, you may continue because you have blind, unquestioning faith in the program and your health guru. If you do that, you might physically breakdown instead of experiencing a breakthrough into optimal health. If you are self-caring, you will question and adjust the program as needed.

Exercise the courage to question and decide what beliefs are worth keeping. *(See the chapter on Belief and Doubt.)*

Optimal living is serious business; it is your happiness and your life. Yet, if you take it too seriously, you suffer. Find dynamic balance between seriousness and play and let go with an open heart and an open, joyful mind.

> *"There's nothing to do, so get on with it."*
> Ram Dass*

## EXERCISE

## Take a Breather

Here is a technique you can practice anytime, anywhere, called "Taking a Breather." It is a moment of presence for shifting from conceptual thinking and reactivity to calm presence, and can help you get out of your head and into your body. Breathers take a few seconds, at most a minute or two. You can take one anytime, anywhere, under any conditions.

- You can do the steps quickly, just touching on each, or you can dwell on one or more of them. At first you can practice for a minute or two so you become used to dropping out of seriousness into calm:
- Sense and adjust your posture so you are relaxed and comfortably erect.
- Feel the weight against your chair or your feet on the ground, the sensations of the air against your skin.
- Subtly smile to yourself.
- Focus your attention, gently but firmly, on the sensations of your breath.
- With each outbreath, experience a subtle sigh, "Aaaaahhhh…" and imagine unnecessary tension leaving your body.
- With each inbreath, take in and circulate clear, bright, invigorating healing energy.
- Observe and allow what is going on in and around you—thoughts, feelings, sensations, sounds, etc.

If you do nothing more than this moment-to-moment informal practice regularly during your day, you will experience a noticeable and pleasant shift.

Try it for 40 days. Every day, make it a point to take a breather from time to time. See what happens.

Take a breather when the phone rings, you get a ping, when you feel a strong emotion, or you realize you are "spacing out" or caught up in obsessive thinking. You can set an alarm to regularly remind yourself to stop and take a moment of presence.

SECTION 2

# Ideals

*"The cyclone derives its power from a calm center. So does a person."*
Norman Vincent Peale

Ideals are goals to be aimed at, standards of perfection. Until the problem of self-imposed stress is solved, choose to be goal oriented and let the goal motivate your work on yourself.

The goal is to approach perfection, to realize the ideals of wellness, living in dynamic balance, and Flow, calmly ready for anything and performing skillfully with competence, kindness, and compassion. The goal is to live in a way that makes the best of your situation, learning and growing from every experience.

CHAPTER 6

# Calm Center

*We come spinning out of nothingness, scattering stars,*
*the stars form a circle . . . and in the center, we dance.*
Rumi*

Central to the peaceful warrior's ideals is equanimity, a sense of calm in the face of anything. It is to be in touch with a *calm center*—a sense of serenity, peace, clarity, and comfort—whether you are in motion or at rest.

Jean-Jacque Rousseau believed our natural state is a neutral and peaceful condition. King David, in Psalm 61, said, "When my heart is overwhelmed, lead me to the rock that is higher than I." Both of these spoke of what we might refer to as a "calm center."

Being centered is being physically and psychologically present, aware of what is going on internally and externally, both completely involved and unattached. It is the peace of quiet joy beneath the waves of the ups and downs you experience during life. It is being comfortable in the moment, doing whatever you are doing.

We can think of that calm center as the eye of a storm where it is calm and peaceful while the winds—emotions, thoughts, chaos, stressful relationships, deadlines—swirl. When we are caught up in the wind, we lose the calm. The eye of the storm is awareness.

Another way to think of being centered is to imagine sitting behind a waterfall. The water (the movement of your thoughts, sensations, and feelings) is roaring down. Behind it you are safe and dry, able to see clearly.

Whether we think of it as the eye of the storm or sitting behind the waterfall, it is the experience that matters. The calm center is not really a center. It is a state of equilibrium, the felt sense of a point that opens into awareness, the platform from which you act most effectively. It is the source of unconditional compassion and kindness. It is home, a place of comfort and refuge. Your center is always available, though it is often covered over by thoughts, conditioning, and other emotions.

In touch with calm, clarity, and peace, you can experience and accept whatever is occurring so you can respond and adjust as required to enable wellness and maintain dynamic balance.

## EXERCISE

### Meditation Technique

To find your center, step back and objectively observe. *(There is more on this in the chapters on "Meditation" and "Mindfulness.")* Stepping back requires practice. It requires both that you train your mind and that you possess a felt sense of what it means to be centered.

There are many ways to attain that felt sense, including meditation practice and remembering moments when you were calmly at peace. Remember "breathers"? Each breather you take is a stepping back.

Serenity, quiet joy, is the underlying feeling when you are centered. Whenever you recognize that you are distracted, reacting, tense, or uneasy, STOP. Take a breather.

To train your mind to step back more easily into your center, practice a more formal meditation* technique. You can read the following instructions aloud and record them, or just read them through to obtain a sense of the technique. Practice them with relaxed effort, kindness to yourself, and patient perseverance:

- Find a comfortable place where you are not likely to be disturbed or distracted.
- Set a timer (5, 10, 15 minutes or more), take your seat, and sit comfortably erect.
- Bring your attention to the sensations of your body—feel your body against the chair or cushion, the air against your skin.
- Take a conscious gentle breath or two.
- Slowly go through your body, touching it with your mind: as you feel your body, bring your attention to the whole body, not just the surface. Feel your head and face. Feel the inside of your mouth, sinuses, and skull. Feel your head balanced on your neck, your shoulders gently dropped back and down. Feel the sensations of your torso, your pelvic area, arms, hands, legs, feet.
- Shift your attention to the sensations of your breath. Notice the sensations wherever it is most prevalent for you, the rising and falling of your chest and abdomen, the air passing through your nostrils.
- For a few moments, breathing in, imagine the breath filling your body, relaxing and energizing it. Breathing out, feel the release of tension, without forcing it.
- Then drop the imagining and just breathe naturally.
- Accept the way you are in this moment.
- Notice any thoughts, feelings, sensations, sounds, smells, visual images—anything that occurs in or around you.
- Just notice.
- Experience thoughts, sensations, feelings, sounds, and anything else that comes up as if they were clouds passing in the sky.
- Notice the desire to think about any of them. Bring attention back to the breath.
- If you fall asleep or become distracted, as soon as you notice it, gently bring your attention back to the sensations of your breath.
- Continue to notice and return.

There will be thinking. Don't worry about it or try to stop it. Just notice the thinking, the thinking about the thinking, feelings, sensations, sounds, visual images—allow anything that comes up in or around you.

Don't worry if you are spacing out, falling asleep, or losing focus. It is natural and will happen. Whenever you notice that you have been lost in thought, asleep, or "spaced-out," bring your attention back to your object of focus, in this case your breath, and begin again, just noticing.

Getting lost is natural. Celebrate the moment of realizing you have been distracted. In that moment, you are mindfully aware.

If the timer rings and your thoughts have experienced non-stop thinking or you realize you have been asleep the whole time, don't give up. Renew your intention and come back next time.

*(There is a chapter in this book, "Training the Mind: Meditation" that describes meditation in some depth. But it is doing it that gives you the sense of what it feels like to rest in your center.)*

_____

CHAPTER 7

# Motivation: Intentions, Goals, and Plans

*"'When someone is seeking,' said Siddhartha, 'it happens quite easily that he only sees the thing he is seeking; that he is unable to find anything, unable to absorb anything, because he . . . is obsessed with his goal. . . . Seeking means to have a goal; but finding means to be free, to be receptive, to have no goal.'"*[5]
Hermann Hesse

After college, I had the underlying values of wanting to be happy with a stable family and a decent job. Then it was the mid-1960s and change was in the air. I became dissatisfied with mindlessly attempting to achieve the American Dream. That dissatisfaction led me to into personal psychology and mystical self-awareness traditions, with the goal of freedom.

It's not that my values were bad in and of themselves. Wanting to achieve success, and applying the effort to achieve it, is fine. Wanting is not the problem. The problem is being attached to getting what you want, when you want it, and becoming so focused on the future goal that you miss the present.

Goals, values, and plans set direction and fuel our efforts. Perseverance is needed to face, overcome, and learn from challenges.

---

[5] Hesse, Hermann, *Siddhartha*, Bantum Books, p. 140.

Stretch goals, shooting for the moon, are healthy, if we realize that the attempt to achieve them may not fully succeed.

> *"Studies show that people are not only more creative when they reach for higher, bigger goals but also more motivated and productive. A 1997 study revealed that after Motorola implemented stretch goals in its management training, engineers were able to develop new products in a tenth of the time that it took previously. Decades later, it still holds true, as Google can attest."*[6]

It is useful to recognize the subtle differences between goals. objectives, and intentions. If you can do this, you are more likely to get what you want and want what you get.

## Intention, Goals, Values

Let's define terms. **Goals** set an unclouded vision of how you would like things to be. **Objectives** apply more specific concrete details to make the vision more vivid and achievable. **Intention** is about a commitment to doing something, in a certain way, with certain values. **Values** are principles or standards you judge as important, such as resilience, adaptability, kindness, compassion, integrity, self-reliance, courage, etc.

For example, your goal might be to go to the beach, sit in the sun, and take some dips in the sea. Your objectives would be about which beach, what time, and for how long. Your intention is to enjoy

---

[6] Main, Kelly, "Google Uses the 2-Plus Method to Ignite Productivity and Fuel Growth without Burnout," Inc.com, https://www.inc.com/kelly-main/google-uses-o2-plus-method-to-ignite-productivity-fuel-growth-without-burnout.html#:~:text=The%20%22O2%2DPlus%22%20method%20is%20another%20example%20of%20Google's,but%20rapidly%20burn%20itself%20out. Accessed April 10, 2023.

some fun and relax, communing with nature. Your values are acceptance, resilience, and adaptability.

If you are dissatisfied when the day turns out to be cloudy and cool, you might not fulfill your intention. You have become attached to your goal. If you change the goals and objectives to include walks along the beach, playing ball, and watching the waves, you can still relax and commune, as you intended.

More broadly, if your intention is wellness, your goal might be to resolve all the issues in the way. Your objectives include being increasingly patient, less reactive, and more able to focus without being distracted.

Setting an intention makes it less likely that you will be so caught up in achieving your objectives that you lose track of what is most important. With wise intention, you are more likely to be satisfied even when things don't go the way you expected them to go.

## Satisfying Your Needs

Needs drive intention. Intention influences behavior.

Abraham Maslow, an expert in human motivation, whose work is a foundation for many practical business leadership models, theorized that all people are motivated to satisfy a hierarchy of needs for physiological safety, security, belonging, recognition, self-actualization, and self-transcendence.

For example, if a person is starving, obtaining food would likely take precedence over becoming socially recognized. That person's goal is to survive.

Physiological safety, security, belonging, recognition, and self-actualization are the worldly needs that are satisfied by working on yourself. According to Maslow, self-transcendence is about identifying with something beyond yourself.

The hierarchy is not rigid. All models and theories are imperfect reflections of the way things are. The levels overlap. For example, a starving person who values cooperative living can overcome the urge to immediately find something to eat at all costs. A person operating on any of the other levels may be motivated by self-transcendence and that motivation would color the way the other needs are experienced.

I am reminded of Primo Levi's assertion that in the Nazi concentration camps "the best all died," often because they shared their food with others and refused to compromise their values.

## Planning

> *"A goal without a plan is just a wish."*
> Antoine de Saint-Exupery

> *"If you fail to plan, you are planning to fail!"*
> Benjamin Franklin

Achieving wellness is an ongoing program that requires planning.

Planning is deciding when and how to proceed to meet goals and objectives. Planning well means accepting that uncertainty is the only certainty. It means visualizing a desired outcome, figuring out how to achieve it, letting go into the process, and creatively adapting as things change.

(The goal of optimal performance and wellness is described in the next chapter, "Performance, Wellness, Dynamic Balance, and Flow.") To realize the goal, plan to change the habits that hold you back by courageously opening your mind.

### EXERCISE

## Intentions, Values, Goals, and Objectives

Reflect on and write down your intentions, values, goals, and objectives. For the objectives, include time frames, for example, practicing meditation practice for 40 days. Make them realistic.

Every so often review them and make any changes you think necessary. Be aware of how you feel when you change them, particularly when you have fallen short. Note the reasons for your successes and shortfalls. Congratulate yourself on your successes and on your resilience and flexibility.

CHAPTER 8

# Performance, Wellness, Dynamic Balance, and Flow

*"All the world's a stage, and all the men and women merely players: they have their exits and their entrances; and one man in his time plays many parts . . ."*
William Shakespeare[7]

Living optimally means performing as best as possible while cultivating the dynamic balance and Flow that enable wellness. This chapter defines what we mean by performance, wellness, Flow, and dynamic balance and their relationship to one another.

## Performance

The word *performance* means both the process of accomplishing an objective and an act or event of entertainment.

Your performance, i.e., the way you live your life, demonstrates how well your solution to the problem of self-imposed stress is working. Your mindset,* skills, experience, environment, and performance influence your performance. You are performing well if you are:

---

[7] If Shakespeare were writing today, he would likely change the word "man" to person.

- sustainably doing the best you can under present conditions even if they are severe, instable, chaotic, surprising, and disorienting,
- able to meet multiple, changing, and often conflicting objectives while managing volatility, uncertainty, complexity, and ambiguity,
- experiencing wellness,
- frequently finding yourself in Flow and dynamic balance, and
- continuously improving.

Consider all life as a play or movie in which we all are performers, directors, writers, and audience. You perform to attain what you need or want, like applause, a wonderful career, a great life partner, being a positive influence, behaving ethically, experiencing contentment, being less reactive and more responsive, and acting with kindness and compassion.

To make performance more challenging, we all can play multiple roles. Everyone—leaders, employees, artists, yogis, spiritual seekers, teachers, students, coaches, independent contractors, soldiers, stay-at-home parents, and care takers—plays multiple roles. Over- or under-identify with any roles and performance suffers. Take a step back to become the executive producer who trusts the director, writers, actors, and crew to do what needs to be done.

## Wellness / Wellbeing

Performing well means intelligently cultivating a supportive, healthy, lifestyle—not just physically healthy but healthy in the sense that all the dimensions of your life (emotions, intellect, body, spirit, relationships, work, finances, and environment) are in dynamic balance.

Wellness is being healthy in the sense that you are practicing a dynamically balanced lifestyle. Dr. Peggy Swarbrick described a wellness lifestyle as having eight interdependent dimensions:

*Emotional:* According to the National Institute of Health, emotional wellness is "the ability to successfully handle life's stresses and adapt to change and difficult times." *(See the chapter on "Working with Emotions.")*

*Intellectual:* Recognizing, applying, and expanding creative abilities, knowledge, and skills. Applying analysis and intuition. *(See the chapters on "View, Belief, and Doubt" and "Wisdom and Spiritual Intelligence.")*

*Physical:* Maintaining a healthy body, balancing physical activity, nutrition, sleep, relaxation, and immune support. *(See the chapter on "Working with the Body.")*

*Spiritual:* Expanding the sense of purpose and meaning in life. It is related to spiritual intelligence, which Stephen Covey considers as the "most fundamental of all the intelligences because it becomes the source of guidance for the others."[8] *(See the chapter on Wisdom and Spiritual Intelligence.)*

*Social:* Having a sense of connection, relationship, and belonging, in a support system. *(See the chapters on "Working in Relationships" and "Community.")*

*Occupational:* Having personal satisfaction and enrichment in work. *(See the chapter on "Working at Work.")*

*Financial:* Having financial conditions based on the knowledge and skills required to plan and manage current and future finances.

---

[8] Covey, Stephen, *The 8th Habit: From Effectiveness to Greatness*, Simon and Schuster, 2004, p. 53.

*Environmental:* Living in an environment that supports well-being and supporting and promoting that environment by behaving in an ecologically conscious way.

## Flow: Performing in the Zone

Earlier we defined "Flow" as being fully engaged, performing as best as you ever have, and at the same time observing it all without thinking about it. Being in Flow, or in the Zone,* as much as possible, is a goal.

According to Mihaly Csikszentmihaly, the Flow experience is a merging of action and awareness; you are aware of what is happening but not thinking about it. If you think about your experience, your performance immediately suffers. You are no longer present; you are looking back or ahead.

Flow occurs when you are undistractedly engaged. There is calm, a distorted sense of time, a loss of ego centeredness. It is as if action is occurring without a doer. It is effortless effort naturally expressing intention, skills, knowledge, and experience.

While Flow is usually associated with high-intensity activities like sports, it can occur whenever you are fully attending to whatever you are doing. You may have experienced Flow while playing ping pong or music, dancing, or giving a presentation, while washing dishes or concentrating on any task, or walking down the street. You can experience Flow even in a heated argument.

Do not expect perfection in experiencing and maintaining Flow. You may experience it for a moment, or more sustainably, infrequently, or frequently. You may not experience it at all. Just keep applying the effort to cultivate mindfulness and concentration until flow becomes part of your experience. *(See the chapters on "Mindfulness" and "Meditation.")*

The secret to Flow is to let go into the movement, notice when you become distracted, and let go again.

# PERFORMANCE, WELLNESS, DYNAMIC BALANCE, AND FLOW

## Dynamic Balance

To be in Flow requires dynamic balance. Dynamic balance is being stable while in motion, flexible, adapting to the moment. There are causes and effects, positives and negatives, hope and fear, activity and rest, friends and foes, happiness and sadness, success and failure, growth and decay, form and emptiness, wisdom and ignorance, disappointments, pain, old age, sickness, and death. To cultivate dynamic balance is to accept it all and blend it with your intentions and values into a lifestyle that suits your situation—your personality, health status, living conditions, and cultural norms.

When the interdependent dimensions of well-being are in dynamic balance, spiritual well-being influences emotional well-being. Emotional well-being is influenced by and influences the social dimension. Physical and environmental well-being influence all the others. Occupational well-being influences and is influenced by emotional and financial well-being. Wellness influences performance and performance influences happiness and wellness.

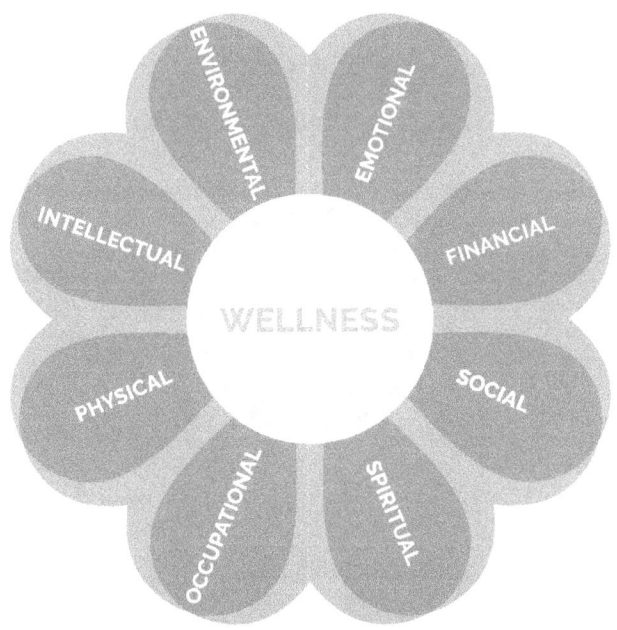

### EXERCISE

## Explore Your Wellness and Performance

Review each of the wellness factors and decide what changes in your life would enhance your wellness and performance.

What gets in the way of putting them into action?

Create a plan. Make it realistic and not a great burden. The plan should address the factors you would like to change, for example, making a budget to increase your financial well-being or committing to physical exercise and diet to address physical well-being. Don't attempt to address everything all at once. Review and prioritize.

Relax. *There's nothing to do, so get on with it.*

CHAPTER 9

# Wellness and Contentment

*"Joy is that kind of happiness that does not depend on what happens."*
David Steindl-Rast*

*"But the fruit of the Spirit is love, joy, peace, patience, kindness, goodness, faithfulness, gentleness, self-control; against such things there is no law."*
Galatians 5:22-23

A sign of wellness is happiness and contentment. This chapter explores happiness: "the experience of joy, contentment, or positive well-being, combined with a sense that one's life is good, meaningful, and worthwhile."[9] Aristotle and the Dalai Lama agree that happiness is a universal goal.

The kind of happiness we are talking about is not the kind that has you dancing around and beaming. The dancing-around kind of happiness is great, but it is temporary. It is conditioned on your mood and external events like obtaining something you like.

The kind of happiness that persists even when you don't get what you want is *not* conditioned by events. It is a deep satisfaction, a

---

[9] Lyubomirsky, Sonja, "The Science and Practice of Happiness Across the Lifespan," Frank B. Roehr Memorial Lecture, University of California Television, https://www.youtube.com/watch?v=MDTi2_PHiiM https://greatergood.berkeley.edu/topic/happiness/definition. Accessed April 10, 2023.

contentment that comes when you are centered, even in the face of change, confusion, imperfection, and disappointment.

Of course, part of living well is to fully enjoy experiences of temporary happiness. *(See the chapter titled "Enjoy Pleasure.")* To do that, it is best to understand how happiness turns to dissatisfaction.

## Conditioned and Unconditional Happiness

Happiness is conditioned by your mindset and setting. It disappears if you try to keep it going when the external events change, you judge it, or when you lose interest. There is discontent if there is a constant pursuit of what you think will make you happy. There is also discontent if what makes you happy makes others unhappy.

Here are some examples of how conditions effect happiness:

- If you are busily involved in something you like, a call from a friend who wants to chat can be annoying. If you are bored and feeling alone, the same call will make you happy.
- When I am fully immersed in an activity I like, I am happy. Then, there is a letdown, a sense of disappointment, when it is over.
- You may take a spoonful of your favorite flavor of ice cream and be happy as you experience the cold, creamy sweetness. Take another spoonful, and then another, driven by the desire for more of that happiness, and it's gone. If you have eaten too much of it, or you didn't have enough, or if you are worried or guilty about ruining your looks or health, then you are unhappy.

There is a story of Siddhartha Gautama before he became the Buddha. He had spent six years strenuously seeking the end of suffering and he had not found it. Frustrated, he asked himself if there was another way. He remembered a childhood experience. Sitting under a tree, he experienced a simple pleasure of contentment.

## WELLNESS AND CONTENTMENT

In that moment, he realized, *Simple happiness is borne of relaxed contemplation.*

> *". . . there's a deeper kind of joy . . .*
> *It's the joy of a deeply flowing river that doesn't*
> *have a lot of ripples on it, or waves,*
> *and this is really the joy of peace.*
> *The Buddha at one time said peace is the greatest happiness.*
> *We might call it a quiet joy, and that quiet joy can be underneath*
> *all the waves, because there will be waves—the ups and downs,*
> *times of exuberance and times when we're feeling low."*
> Joseph Goldstein[10]

## Don't Worry, Be Happy

> *"Do your best, then don't worry, be happy."*
> Meher Baba

Worry, obsessively thinking about the future, replaces contentment with anxiety. We worry that a pleasant experience is or will be over, that an unpleasant sensation won't go away or will become worse, or that something terrible will happen.

It is easy to say, "Don't worry," but it is not easy to stop. Habits like worrying are hard to break. But mindful of them, you can soften their effect. You can make them reminders to be mindfully persistent in making the effort to change your mind.

When you realize you are worrying, step back to presence. If the worrying doesn't stop, shift into figuring out what to do to handle whatever you are worrying about.

---

[10] Goldstein, Joseph, "Joseph Goldstein on Easing Self-Judgement and Finding Joy," *Tricycle: The Buddhist Review*, Tricycle.org, July 15, 2021, https://tricycle.org/trikedaily/joseph-goldstein-self-judgement-joy/.

## EXERCISE
## **Cultivating Contentment**

Note in your journal the things that make you happy.

Can you be okay, calm, and centered when you don't obtain them?

How about when you realize things are changing in a way that threatens your physical safety, security, and power, poking holes in your expectations and beliefs? When in chronic pain? Or when your lover walks away?

How long does it take to recover from discontentment? What speeds the recovery process?

Does acceptance result in greater peace and contentment? If not, what is standing in the way?

CHAPTER 10

# Ready for Anything: Cognitive Readiness

*"The bad news is you're falling through the air,
nothing to hang on to, no parachute.
The good news is there's no ground."*
Chögyam Trungpa

*"How does it feel, how does it feel? To be on
your own, with no direction home?"*
Bob Dylan

Contentment in the face of change and uncertainty comes when you are ready for anything with expectations that no matter what happens you will be able to handle it.

This chapter describes the ability to be cognitively ready to effectively confront and successfully address anything that comes up. *(The chapters on "Mental Models," and "Working with Emotions" provide insights and methods for building cognitive readiness.)*

There is an old curse, "May you live in interesting times." Interesting times are times that capture your attention. When everything is just going along, you can be lulled to sleep. When things become interesting, you wake up. If you are intent on living as well as you can, waking up is a good thing. If you are intent upon staying comfortably asleep, then "interesting times" is a curse.

Are you living in interesting times? In your experience, are things changing more rapidly, becoming increasingly complex and uncertain? Is there an increasing sense of uncertainty? Do you feel stressed by it or energized by it? Or do you take it as it comes because it is normal?

## Be Cognitively Ready

Being cognitively ready means to be able to perform effectively in the face of uncertainty and ambiguity resulting from uncontrollable change.

Cognitive readiness was defined by the U.S. military as "the mental preparation (including skills, knowledge, abilities, motivations, and personal dispositions) an individual needs to establish and sustain competent performance in the complex and unpredictable environment..."[11] The environment they were talking about was battle: lives are at stake; there is chaos and unpredictability. While our lives might not be as dramatically at stake as in battle, sometimes it seems as if they are when meaningful change or transformation occurs.

Wellness requires the ability to thrive knowing there will be change and that we don't know *how things will turnout*—what health issues, relationship changes, or any of many other life-changing events will occur.

## Changing Times

The condition of instable, chaotic, surprising, and disorienting situations is described with two terms, which are acronyms: VUCA and BANI. VUCA (<u>v</u>olatility, <u>u</u>ncertainty, <u>c</u>omplexity and <u>a</u>mbiguity)

---

[11] Morrison, John W., and Fletcher, J.D., Cognitive Readiness, Institute for Defense Analyses, 2002. Download at http://www.dtic.mil/cgi-bin/GetTRDoc?AD=ADA417618 , pp. 1-3.

is normal, though if it is not expected, it can be disturbing. BANI (**b**rittleness, **a**nxiety, **n**on-linearity, and **i**ncomprehensibility) is extreme VUCA.

- **B**rittleness refers to no longer being able to rely on experience, being in a new and uncharted situation. It is brittle because rigidity sets in, wanting to hold onto the way things are or go back to the way things were. Brittle things break easily.
- **A**nxiety is caused by facing the unknown and lacking control. Beyond anxiety there is existential fear: "Will I and those I love survive?" "Will life be miserable?" Brittleness brings anxiety.
- **N**on-linearity feeds anxiety. It refers to the realization that we are in a highly complex process with multiple dimensions interacting and moving in multiple directions that we can't control. It is high complexity.
- **I**ncomprehensibility refers to the reality that we can't wrap the cognitive mind around what is happening. The cognitive mind is linear; non-linearity requires letting go into intuition.

BANI causes worry, stress, and reactivity. These situations are personal threats to safety and security—for example, losing a job, or facing threats to global stability.

Yuval Harari, in his book *Homo Deus: A Brief History of Tomorrow*, says that based on current trends, it is becoming increasingly evident that the future will not be a linear extension of the past. He believes there is a wide array of alternative possibilities. Artificial intelligence, neuroscience, advances in medicine and medical technology, extreme income inequality, the rise of authoritarianism, ecological shifts, and more can lead us into an uncharted future.

For example, imagine a future in which there is a large class of people for whom there is no productive work and a class of upgraded humans who enjoy the advantages of the latest technologies to enhance themselves and their offspring using genetic engineering and advanced automation. The future can be rosy for all, if health and prosperity is shared, or a dark time for the former—the many led by an elite class of self-serving super humans living in protected gardens of delight.

While this scenario does indeed sound alarming, non-linear, incomprehensible volatility and uncertainty are nothing new. Unpredictable change has been with us since the dawn of time. In the past, it may have been easier to hide from it. Today, it is in our face. I do best when I find my center and remember that I can accept what I cannot change and can plan and act to influence the future to some extent. Self-aware, active, relaxed, centered, allowing, ready for anything, I can accept whatever happens and let go into doing the best I can do, regardless of the circumstances.

## How to Cultivate Readiness

You can cultivate cognitive readiness by returning to your calm center, accepting emotional responses without letting them drive your behavior or become so strong that they distort your perception. This requires effort. The section on "Practices" gives you the tools and techniques to do this. The "Mindset" section provides concepts to provide you with a platform that supports the practices.

You can shield yourself from unnecessary change, but you cannot stop it. And, any shield can be broken. A good practice is to cultivate your ability to stay calm and competent when faced with VUCA/BANI.

## EXERCISE
## Cultivate Cognitive Readiness

Identify the challenges in your life that require you to exercise cognitive readiness—changes you are experiencing (or anticipating) that trigger anxiety or other challenging emotions.

Choose one situation and imagine how you can accept being out of control.

Write in your journal about the way you feel when you are faced with unstable, out-of-control situations.

CHAPTER 11

# Skillful Action

*"You must be the change you wish to see in the world."*
Mahatma Gandhi

*"Fires can't be made with dead embers, nor can enthusiasm be stirred by spiritless men. Enthusiasm in our daily work lightens effort and turns even labor into pleasant tasks."*
James Baldwin

This chapter summarizes the recipe for making the best of a situation. We will discuss setting values and intentions to act skillfully to accomplish your goals—centered, well, content, and ready for anything.

In Buddhist thought, skillful action boils down to acting, speaking, and earning a living in such a way that you "do no harm," and if you can, to help by being of service to yourself and others. In Western spiritual traditions, right action is expressed in the Golden Rule: "Do unto others as you would have others do unto you." In the end, both traditions focus on ethical behavior.

In a practical sense, skillful action is action that gets you what you want. If you value lovingkindness and compassion, then there is no conflict between ethical behavior and practical action. If what you want is not moderated by those values, you might get what you want but not like what you get.

Unskillful action, on the other hand, violates values and does not accomplish goals. It results from a closed mind that seeks to block change and stick to rigid ideas of how things should be, fighting against or hiding away in denial and depression from anything that is in your way.

## How Will You Act?

In "interesting times," when current events do not predictably follow past trends, skillful action means being resilient and responsive as opposed to reactive, so you can surf the waves of change.

*Resilience* is commonly defined as the quality of quick recovery from difficulties. It is the ability to spring back into shape—though, in our context, we never really spring back into anything. Resilience is about using difficulties as fuel for growth.

*Responsiveness* is "responding especially readily and sympathetically to appeals, efforts, influences, etc."[12] It is the quality of adapting thoughtfully. This may be immediate or measured and well thought out. For example, a well-trained police officer will respond with action that fits the situation; she will let her training rather than her fear or bias inform her. Sometimes the right response is to shoot first, sometimes not. Sometimes doing nothing is the right response.

*Reactivity* is immediate and without conscious thought, like a knee jerk. It is the quality that untrained warriors exhibit; they flare up in anger or retreat in fear. Reactive behavior is driven by the emotions. It tends to be self-serving. While sometimes it is lifesaving, most situations call for responsiveness.

The following definition strikes at the heart of both responsiveness and resilience:

---

[12] Dictionary.com

> *"Resilience is the ability to respond to extreme stress with extraordinary competence. Numerous studies cite qualities such as intelligence, emotional flexibility, independence, sensitivity, curiosity, and the willingness to reach out for love and support as central components of resilience.*
>
> *"Other protective factors include introspection, altruism, self-awareness, a sense of humor, optimism in the face of adversity, and a willingness to rely upon one's own inner resources . . . resilient people believed they had the ability to exercise some measure of control no matter how dire the circumstances."*[13]

According to the U.S. Army's resilience program, "The six resilience competencies outlined by the program are self-awareness, self-regulation, optimism, mental agility, strengths of character, and connection, and are the building blocks of improving resilience within oneself."[14]

## Exerting Effort, Accepting and Letting Go

Hopefully by now you have comprehended the idea we keep coming back to: **the foundation for overcoming self-imposed stress and living optimally is to find your calm center, actively accept things as they are, and then let go into doing what you can to realistically pursue wellness.**

It takes balanced effort to act skillfully. Too much and you add unnecessary stress, too little effort and you don't obtain the results you are shooting for.

---

[13] Noble, Dr. Kathleen D., "Spiritual Intelligence," *Advance Development* Vol. 9, 2000.
[14] Ryan, Staff Sgt. Matthew D., "Master Reslience Trainers, Army.mil, January 23, 2014, https://www.army.mil/article/118666/master_resilience_trainers.

It is as if you were in a fast-moving river, heading for a waterfall. You cannot stop the river. Swimming with heroic effort against the current will tire you out and get you nowhere. Holding onto a stone or branch offers only temporary relief. Not doing anything and over the falls you go. Swim diagonally across the current and you increase your chances of reaching the riverbank before the falls.

Similarly, in sailing, sailing straight into the wind will not propel you to your destination. To go against the wind, you travel at an angle as close to the wind's direction as possible, tacking back and forth, zig-zagging to move your boat to where you want to be. Use the wind and your sailing skills to achieve your goal. If the wind stops, waiting patiently is the best you can do unless you are in possession of oars or a motor.

These examples reinforce the idea that the ability to skillfully respond rather than react is a life saver. While there are no guarantees, going with the flow is the way to go if you want to conserve energy and be able to achieve your goals.

The next two sections are guidelines for cultivating the concepts and methods that will help you become calm and centered so you can let skillful action flow naturally, accepting the fact that you are not in control of the current or the wind, but do possess the power to try to direct your life.

And remember to not take it too seriously. Lighten up.

*"A smile is the beginning of peace."*
Mother Teresa

EXERCISE

## Skillful Action

Think about how it would be if you were a guitarist trying to tune your instrument. If you make the strings too tight, what will happen? If you don't make them tight enough, will you achieve the sound you want?

Note how you can apply this metaphor to a particular situation in your life—for example, finding a job, working out, resolving a conflict, or losing or gaining weight. What is "skillful action" in your situation? How do over and under efforting affect the outcome?

SECTION 3

# Mindset

*"Mind precedes all mental states. Mind is their chief; they are all mind-wrought. If with a pure mind a person speaks or acts, happiness follows him like his never-departing shadow."*
Dhammapada

This section explores the concepts that, together with the practices in the next section such as meditation, working with your body, emotions, work situation, and relationships—form the solution to the problem of self-imposed stress. Each chapter explores various aspects of how the way you think, and the way you perceive the world and where you fit in it, affects your life. While the topics are conceptual, the emphasis is on going beyond concept to experience.

In the above quote, the *Dhammapada's* "mind" refers to our mindset—the way we feel and think and the concepts that influence our behavior. Both experiential knowledge and concepts are indispensable to gain meaningful knowledge. Concepts are thoughts or ideas that describe something. Conceptual thinking involves the brain's frontal cortex, which controls our executive function and analytical and intuitive thinking. Executive function enables skills such as self-regulation, time management, planning, focusing attention, remembering instructions, and organizing.

Experience, on the other hand, is the realm of feelings, emotions, and physical sensations.

A critical part of wellness is to objectively observe your own mindset, and be able to adjust it at will to support your own wellness.

## Burn the Boat

Views, methods, and models are concepts about the workings of your world, and also of your mind—with its sensations, thoughts, and emotions. Your conceptual understanding influences your work on yourself. For example, the concept that you can go beyond your limitations motivates doing it.

But, if we take these concepts too seriously, they can stand in our way. The concepts about how to live optimally are like a boat to take you from where you are across an imagined ocean to a better place. When you reach the other shore, burn the boat. You don't need to carry it around with you. It has served its purpose.

Of course, there is no other shore, no ocean. The idea is to use concepts as part of the method to go beyond concepts to experience. The path is not about simply moving from one place to another. It is about dissolving the things that stand in the way of realizing peaceful presence, here and now.

Peaceful presence is another face of being calmly centered. To be peaceful is to be equanimous, undisturbed by chaos and strife. Presence is the quality of being present and attentive to what is happening in the moment, instead of being caught up in extraneous thoughts or lost in your phone. It is associated with having a dignified, composed nature.

Until the dissolving of the things that stand in the way is complete, take care of your boat.

*"Words! The Way is beyond language."*
Sengstan, Third Zen Patriarch*

CHAPTER 12

# Awareness

*"A sense of the universe, a sense of the all, the nostalgia which seizes us when confronted by nature, beauty, music—these seem to be an expectation and awareness of a Great Presence."*
Pierre Teilhard de Chardin

Awareness has been mentioned several times and is a critical part of wellness. This chapter defines and explores awareness, which is what we experience when we go beyond "thinking about" to non-conceptual knowing. It is the felt sense of being centered and letting go in Flow.

Awareness is always available, though we might not be conscious of it. We can be aware of thinking and aware of thinking about thinking. In fact, right now you are probably aware that you are reading, thinking about what you are reading, and aware that you are thinking about the fact that you are thinking. That awareness is a subtle knowing. It is *not* merely thinking about something. Awareness is often compared to a mirror. Thoughts and everything else, are occurring as images in the mirror.

Awareness can only be experienced. Thinking about something separates us from it and takes us out of the immediate experience. Thinking about awareness lets us know that awareness exists, but it is *not* awareness.

A taste of awareness is needed to tell the difference between awareness and intellectually or conceptually knowing. Something wakes you up. It could be a bell rung while you are quietly sitting or stumbling while walking. Note the moment before you react. Maybe as you read that "awareness is not thinking about something," there was a moment that you were *aware* before you started thinking about it.

Seek awareness with conceptual thinking and you won't find it. Stop looking for it and it will appear. Mindfulness meditation and taking breathers increase the frequency of waking up to awareness and enable you to stay awake longer.

## Awakening

Awakening to awareness:

> *". . . gives rise to an indescribable joy.*
> *We have experienced for ourselves that awakening is a genuine option, for us and for everyone else—how wonderful! The heartfelt wish that everyone may awaken to true freedom is born in us and consumes us to the point where our attachment and delusion seem to dissolve naturally. All the while, we see the world for what it is, . . ."*[15]
> Chokyi Nyima Rinpoche

If awareness is a subtle, ever-present quality of mind of which we may be unaware, awakening is the recognition of awareness. Awakening happens suddenly, although there is generally a gradual process of experiencing brief moments of awareness. Each of these experiences, like awakening itself, is spontaneous and immediate—like an "aha moment."

---

[15] Rinpoche, Choky Nyima, "The Secret Strength of Sadness," Tricycle: The Buddhist Review, Tricycle.org, June 27, 2018, https://tricycle.org/trikedaily/chokyi-nyima-rinpoche-sadness/?utm_source=Tricycle&utm_campaign=83cdf27833-3teachings_22_02_24_NS&utm_medium=email&utm_term=0_1641abe55e-83cdf27833-307270717

When we are not awake to awareness, it is because we are distracted by life, thoughts, and feelings. We may be complacent, not motivated to think beyond "what is." We may be lost in fantasy, obsession, or worry.

For example, Jimmy, an intelligent, capable professional, is convinced he cannot live with the anxiety of facing the uncertainty of an upcoming operation. He obsesses about all the negative possibilities, the pain of recovery, the possibility of dying on the operating table, or becoming a vegetable from the anesthesia. His anxiety increases. He says, "I can't stand it." Yet he is "standing" it.

If Jimmy steps back and becomes aware that his obsessive thinking causes his anxiety, there is a chance he can calm down and accept his situation. That awakening will not make the operation and recovery pleasant. It might not stop the thinking. However, it will contribute to a greater sense of peace because it puts space around the feelings rather than being completely lost in and reactive to them.

Knowing the difference between being awake and asleep, with the intention to be awake, with practice, we will "wake up" more frequently and stay awake longer, until awakening is naturally part of everyday life. *Celebrate awakening each time it happens.*

## Self-Awareness: Who Are You?

*"Be at least as interested in what goes on inside*
*you as what happens outside.*
*If you get the inside right, the outside will fall into place."*
Eckhart Tolle

Self-awareness is a special kind of awareness. It is one of the three parts of the simple solution to the problem of self-imposed stress, along with acceptance and letting go. There is no single accepted definition of self-awareness, but the following observation is helpful:

> *"For example, some see it [self-awareness] as the ability to monitor our inner world, whereas others label it as a temporary state of self-consciousness. Still others describe it as the difference between how we see ourselves and how others see us.*
>
> *"Across the studies we examined, two broad categories of self-awareness kept emerging. The first, which we dubbed* internal self-awareness, *represents how clearly we see our own values, passions, aspirations, fit with our environment, reactions (including thoughts, feelings, behaviors, strengths, and weaknesses), and impact on others. We've found that internal self-awareness is associated with higher job and relationship satisfaction, personal and social control, and happiness; it is negatively related to anxiety, stress, and depression.*
>
> *"The second category,* external self-awareness, *means understanding how other people view us, in terms of those same factors listed above. Our research shows that people who know how others see them are more skilled at showing empathy and taking others' perspectives."*[16]

Self-awareness is knowing who or what we are, our goals and intentions, our strengths and weaknesses. It's knowing the way the mind operates, our inner workings, and how these affect our behavior. As the foundation for our emotional and social intelligence, self-awareness enables self-management and our ability to choose how to respond rather than to react.

## Who Are You?

Self-awareness exposes that who we think we are, our ego,* is the continuous appearance of thoughts, feelings, physical sensations,

---

[16] Eurich, Tasha, "What Self-Awareness Really Is and How to Cultivate It," *Harvard Business Review,* hrb.org, January 4, 2018, https://hbr.org/2018/01/what-self-awareness-really-is-and-how-to-cultivate-it.

and concepts driven by our thoughts, experiences, and conditioning. This awareness confronts us with one of the more difficult realities to accept: there is no solid self, even though who we think we are seems so real and solid. This theme appeared earlier as we looked at life as a play in which we play multiple roles.

At first reading, my editor commented, "The statement that there is no solid self seems like a pretty dogmatic assertion, with no support."

My response was, "I think it is objectively true. The reader who is confronted with this concept needs to validate it for themselves, not to believe but to know for themselves, based on analysis and experience.

On a physical level, our bodies, including our brains, are constantly changing. Every experience changes us by leaving an imprint, which then creates change in behavior and mindset. Am I the same person I was when I was four years old? My body is different, the way I think is different, my physical capabilities are different, I have had experience. Yet there is a thread that can be followed that ties a life together. Is that thread the self?

The idea that there is no solid self does not mean that the ego, our self, is unreal or is something to be eliminated. It doesn't mean that there is no soul, but we won't get into that question. It means that we do better if we see the self for what it is: a constantly changing process as opposed to an object, a verb instead of a noun.

Do not reject or try to rid yourself of your ego (not that you could even if you wanted to). And where would you be without it? Put the ego in its place, take loving care of it, and use it well as a vehicle for living in the world.

It is a relief when you are aware that your ego is ever-changing and is made up of all your personas, including the one that is mindfully observing the observer. You can stop wasting energy on trying to make your ego last forever, or on holding onto a fixed sense of who you are. You can use the ego instead of letting the ego use you. You can let go and experience Flow.

Remember self-awareness. Who or what is it that is observing, understanding, and directing the ego self? And who or what is observing that self? Experiencing awareness while optimally playing out life is the foundation for wellness and optimal living..

*(The chapters on "Mindfulness," "Belief," "Mental Models," and "Wisdom" explore the concepts that help to understand the meaning of no solid self. The chapter on "Meditation" presents the principal method for moving from concept to experience and validating the premise that there is no solid self.)*

### EXERCISE
## Self-Awareness

Take note of any moments of awareness before conceptual thinking begins, and of the moment when you start thinking about your experience.

Note the felt sense, the physical experience, of moments of happiness, anxiety, excitement, or any emotion.

If you are open to a challenge, try the following method for experiencing awareness beyond concept. Ask, "Who Am I?" and then, "Who's asking?" Each time you find an answer, ask, "Who am I?" again. Don't look for an answer. Just seed the questions and see where the process takes you. If it makes you too anxious, relax, stop asking, and explore the feeling.

Some find this exercise scary since it directly confronts one's sense of self. Don't worry. You can simply not do it, but once you start, it is hard to stop . . . until it no longer bothers you that you may not be who you thought you were.

CHAPTER 13

# Feelings and Perception

*"The best and most beautiful things in the world
cannot be seen or even touched.
They must be felt with the heart."*
Helen Keller

*"Is it really possible to tell someone else what one feels?"*
Leo Tolstoy, *Anna Karenina*

When we are aware, we experience physical sensations, feelings, and thoughts before we start thinking about them. This chapter focuses on the felt sense of sensations and feelings as objects of mindfulness and the way your perceptions of them influence your behavior.

The key point is to be mindful enough to listen to your body's messages, in order to overcome reactivity and cultivate responsiveness. *(See the chapters on "Mental Models," "Making the Best of Pain," "Working with the Body," and, "Working with the Emotions" for how to apply the understanding of feelings and perceptions.)*

## The Quality of Experiences

Feelings.

In the way we commonly use the word, "*. . . feelings are high-level responses which provide a mental and perceptual representation of what is physically happening inside our bodies*"[17]

Our emotional responses result from our feelings and the way we perceive them.

We receive a continuous flow of feeling experiences resulting from contact with a sense object—a sound, visual image, touch, smell, or thought. We perceive them as degrees of the primary sensations of being pleasant, unpleasant, or neutral. Neutral experiences are barely noticed. They are neither pleasant nor unpleasant, so they don't grab our attention as the pleasant and unpleasant feelings do.

> *"Modern neuroscience confirms that everything that registers in the brain is assigned some negative or positive valence. The primary feeling tone comes first. Then, born out of this simple feeling tone, there arises a whole array of secondary feelings, all the emotions we are familiar with, from joy and anger to fear and delight.*
>
> *'Working with the primary feelings is a direct route to enlightenment,' explained one of my Burmese teachers. The stream of primary feelings is always with us, but we often have the mistaken notion that life is not supposed to be this way.*
>
> *We secretly believe that if we can act just right, then our stream of feelings will be pleasant and there will be no pain, no loss. So, when a painful experience arises, we try to get rid*

---

[17] Tonhaque, Danique, "Cognitive Neuroscience: Emotions," *Behavioral Research Blog*, Noldus.com, November 21, 2019, https://www.noldus.com/blog/cognitive-neuroscience-emotions#:~:text=Emotions%20are%20a%20brief%20episode,physically%20happening%20inside%20our%20bodies.

*of it, and when a pleasant experience arises, we try to grasp it. When a neutral experience arises, we tend to ignore it.*"[18]

In life, we experience pleasure, pain, and suffering. Aware of our reactions to these feelings, we can step back and become responsive. Pleasure and pain are still there; they are inevitable. Suffering is optional. This principle is illustrated by the parable of two arrows: the first arrow is the pain of an injury, the second arrow is all the tension, angst, anger, and depression that makes you suffer. You can avoid the second arrow.

*(See the chapter on "Mindful of Process" to see how the inner workings of our mind operates as a process triggered by direct experience that results in behavior.)*

## Perception Is Relative

Feelings are physical; perceptions are mental reflections influenced by the feelings and the setting. For example, on a chilly night, there is a fire. We feel its warmth; the sensation is perceived as pleasant. It brings past experiences of pleasant warmth to mind; we catalogue the new experience in our mind, *Fire on a chilly night is good*. We want more of it, so we keep it going. We start a wood pile, so we are ready for the next chilly night. We talk about the experience. We are conscious of the whole interplay among the senses.

Change the setting and everything changes. It's a hot night, and the fire now elicits different sensations and a whole new scenario. Same fire, different setting, perceptions, and behavior.

With practice, we can objectively observe our feelings and perceptions. Then we can graciously accept all feelings with equanimity—"mental calmness, composure, and evenness of

---

[18] Kornfield, Jack. *The Wise Heart: Buddhist Psychology for the West*. Rider, 2008.

temper, especially in a difficult situation"[19]—accepting the good, bad, and neutral.

Feelings are to be felt. Acceptance is a base for action. Equanimity is not indifference.

*(See the chapters on "Making the Best of Pain" and "Enjoy Pleasure" for tips on how to avoid suffering.)*

---

### EXERCISE
## Mindfulness of Feelings while Eating

Do this mindfulness exercise for a few minutes at each meal. If you are with others, there is no need for them to know what you are doing. Be subtle about it. No stress, no thinking, just feeling and observing with five percent or so of your attention.

Taste something. Note your contact with the food—seeing it, smelling it, bringing it to your mouth, tasting it. Note the initial feeling of pleasure, or pain, before you label it. Feel the sensations of the food in your body and the feeling tone of pleasant or unpleasant.

---

[19] Oxford Languages, https://languages.oup.com/google-dictionary-en/

CHAPTER 14

# Love

*"Love is the bridge between you and everything.
Some say there is a door that opens from one to another.
But if there is no wall, there is no need for door or window."*
Rumi

*"There is an extremely powerful force that, so far, science has not found a formal explanation to. It is a force that includes and governs all others and is even behind any phenomenon operating in the universe and has not yet been identified by us. This universal force is LOVE."*[20]
Albert Einstein

This chapter explores love and reinforces the connection between feelings, emotions, perceptions, and relationships. The mindset we maintain about love is special. It sets a stage for how we operate in the world.

Mindfulness of feelings will put us in touch with the feelings surrounding love. Much has been said about love in songs, poems, speeches, quotes, and media. Concepts and even poetry fall far short

---

[20] Nakash, Josia, "Einstein to His Daughter on the Universal Force of Love," ThriveGlobal.com, https://thriveglobal.com/stories/einstein-letter-to-his-daughter-on-the-universal-force-of-love/. Accessed April 10, 2023.

of the experience. *(See the chapters on "Working with Emotions" and "Working in Relationships" for methods related to the subject of love.)*

While it may be useful to ponder love with the thinking mind, like awareness, it is beyond concept. On a biological level, love is critical to well-being and exists in the realm of the *heart*,* the emotions, and spirituality.

There are many varieties of love: love in relationships and love as a force in nature, romantic and platonic love, love of things, love of people, love of self, conditional and unconditional love, love as a universal presence.

When we think love is a limited commodity, we run after it and try to hold onto it. And then when we find it in a romance or in a fervent love of country, we are never really satisfied. We create conditions—"I'll love you if . . ." We limit our love, allowing human failings like jealousy and possessiveness to cloud our experience of being in love.

Teachings from multiple traditions tell us to open ourselves to the universal force of love, an ever-present and unconditional ocean of love. When we are in touch with that boundless, unconditional love, we can truly love ourselves, our romantic partners, and everyone else. This ocean of love is another label for the unknowable and unbounded expanse of awareness, God, or any of the other attempts at describing the indescribable.

## Opening to Love

Whether it is to love of a romantic object or to universal love, opening ourselves up to love can be challenging. Some people's self-image makes them feel unworthy of being loved. Some are threatened by the vulnerability they feel when they open to loving another—will they be rejected and abandoned, or will they disappear? We put up a shield to protect our heart.

To experience love, lower your shield and risk being lost in the experience. But be careful and kind to yourself. *(See the chapter on "Working in Relationships" to read about the way love informs and enables healthy relationships.)*

## EXERCISE
## Explore Love in Your Life

What is the felt sense when you think you are unloved? When you are in love? When you feel loved? When you love?

Consider the following quotes one at a time and reflect. Note the thoughts and feelings they bring up in you.

> *"This is my commandment, that ye love one another, as I have loved you"*[21]
> Jesus to His Disciples

> *"We can reject everything else: religion, ideology, all received wisdom. But we cannot escape the necessity of love and compassion. This, then, is my true religion, my simple faith. In this sense, there is no need for temple or church, for mosque or synagogue, no need for complicated philosophy, doctrine, or dogma. Our own heart, our own mind, is the temple.'*
> H.H. The Dalai Lama

> *"Love clears the mind of the thick fog of desire, anger, and ignorance. Love is like the sun that burns through the fog, dissolving it, until only vast openness and clarity remain. When nothing but

---

[21] John 15:12; John 13:34–35

*boundless openness and lucidity remain, we come face to face with the basic nature of all phenomena beyond concepts."*[22]
Chokyi Nyima Rinpoche

*"In romantic love, you fall in love with someone, and you say, 'I am in love with him,' or, 'I am in love with her,' meaning that person is my connection to the place in myself where I am love . . . Because when I come near you, I feel that place in myself and I don't feel it unless I'm around you; I am in love with you."*[23]
Ram Dass

*"Unconditional love . . . is part of our deep inner being. It is . . . a state of being. It's not, 'I love you' for this or that reason, not, 'I love you if you love me.' It is love for no reason, love without an object."*
Ram Dass

---

[22] Rinpoche, Chökyi Nyima, "The Secret Strength of Sadness," *The Buddhist Review,* Tricycle.org, June 27, 2018, https://tricycle.org/article/chokyi-nyima-rinpoche-sadness/

[23] Dass, Ram, "What Are the Different Levels of Being in Love?" Ramdass.org, https://www.ramdass.org/different-levels-in-love/. Accessed April 19, 2023.

CHAPTER 15

# Mindfulness

*"Mindfulness means paying attention in a particular way, on purpose, in the present moment, and non-judgmentally."*
Jon Kabat-Zinn

Whether it is to cultivate awakening or to be more conscious of feelings and perceptions, mindfulness is an indispensable quality. If you find that you are prone to "spacing out," being easily distracted and reactive, becoming lost in thought or feelings, you do well to become more mindful.

In this chapter, we define mindfulness and describe its place as a natural part of daily life. *(In the chapter on "Meditation,"\* we explore what meditation is how to use it to cultivate greater mindfulness.)*

Mindfulness\* is witnessing anything and everything, including the witnessing itself, and the witnessing of the witnessing. It is a *subtle stepping back,* a natural and practical quality of mind that objectively observes the arising of sensations, thoughts, feelings, emotions, and concepts without the filters of personal beliefs, biases, and preferences. Objective observation enables awareness, emotional and social intelligence, healthy relationships, open-mindedness, courage, and calm competence.

If you have experienced driving or walking somewhere, arriving at your destination, and having no memory of the trip, you know the difference between being and not being mindful. During that ride you were on autopilot. Mindfulness was suspended. Any event—hitting a pothole, an alarm alerting you that you are drifting out of your lane, being cut off by another driver—will *wake you up*, bring you back to mindfulness.

Being mindful is *not* reflecting on, thinking about, contemplating, or analyzing. It is witnessing, moment to moment, *while* actively immersed in whatever you are experiencing. With practice, it becomes effortless and unobtrusive, as in the Flow experience. Mindfulness informs your working memory, your ability to adjust behavior, and your ability to control your thoughts, and attention.

Mindfulness is not a cure-all; it takes more than observing to sustain wellness. Just being aware of obstacles without understanding them and doing something thing about them does *not* overcome them. Just watching yourself going down a rabbit hole of obsessive thinking does not stop the thinking. But being mindfully aware of what is happening is an essential starting point for responsiveness. If you are not mindful, it is likely you will be reactive, driven by habits, biases, attachments, aversions, conditioning, and neuroses.*

## EXERCISE

### A Subtle Stepping Back

Right now, are you experiencing a quality of knowing that you are reading, and of the thoughts, feelings, sensations, and concepts that are arising and passing away?

How has this question changed your attention and experience of the reading?

## Expectations and Intention

Witnessing the continuous movement of internal and external events, you gain insight and awareness, knowing that everything is changing in a river of causes and effects. Experiencing everything that arises in and around you as something that can be observed, you no longer identify with thoughts and feelings and are no longer easily distracted by them. Attachments drop away. Unnecessary stress is relieved.

But don't expect miraculous breakthroughs (though they may happen). Don't expect to be living blissfully in Flow just because you went to a workshop or retreat and practiced mindfulness meditation for a few months. Mindfulness, as stated previously, is *not* a miracle cure-all. It is one eighth of the Buddhist Eight-fold Path to Enlightenment; the other elements are wise intention and understanding, skillful action, speech and livelihood, concentration, and effort. Mindfulness will not stop thoughts and feelings, though as you become more conscious of them your relationship to them will change. You see them as interesting temporary phenomena.

Cultivating mindfulness takes persistent patient effort, support, and self-acceptance because it is difficult to break the old habits that get in the way—attachment, worry, obsessive thinking, sleepiness and laziness, and unskillful doubt.

Mindfulness is a tool. Saints, assassins, and self-serving leaders all apply it to achieve their goals. Goals and values make the difference. Studies show that mindfulness alone has a limited impact on the kind of behavior that benefits others.[24] They also show that there may be side effects like anxiety, depression, and disassociation as mindfulness brings buried thoughts and feelings to the surface and confronts you with the reality of impermanence, uncertainty, and the absence of a solid self.

---

[24] Pfattheicher , Stefan, Schindler, Simon, "When It Really Counts: Investigating the Relation between Trait Mindfulness and Actual Prosocial Behavior," May 25, 2021, PubMed, https://pubmed.ncbi.nlm.nih.gov/34054263/

This is where courageous and skillful warriorship comes into play. If you are not ready to confront buried thoughts and feelings, you can choose to go slow, using techniques for working with your body, emotions, breath, relationships, sound, and work situation. *(We will look at this in more depth in the "Practices" section.)*

## No Need to Be a *Meditator* to Meditate

Everyone is mindful, to a degree. You can use the mind training of meditation exercises to purposefully cultivate and fine tune mindfulness. To practice meditation, you don't have to become a formal "meditator," sitting on a cushion and going to retreats. *("Breathers" in the exercise following Chapter 5 and the exercise in the "Calm Center" chapter are meditation techniques that cultivate mindfulness.)*

### EXERCISE
# Mindfulness in Daily Life

Reflect on the following examples and questions to give you a sense of where mindfulness fits in your day-to-day experience:

Cut off in traffic, anger arises. *Mindful* of the anger, you experience and witness it. You take a breath and drive on, or you observe yourself reacting, pounding your steering wheel, ranting, and raving. *Unmindful*, you get lost in the reaction.

Consider the way you pay attention to the act of driving a nail into a wall. There is a purposeful attention to what you are doing. It is not forced, but there is unmistakable evidence of objectively attending to what is going on. You are present, focused, and attentive. If you lose attention, you will hit yourself with the hammer. If you force the attention, you will hit yourself with the hammer or miss the nail.

Are you more mindful when speaking to someone you think is an "important" person, say on an interview, vs. talking to a server in a restaurant?

How is your attention when you are walking to work or during a break? Are you mindful of your movement, thoughts, and where you are placing your attention, or are you spaced out, lost in thought?

CHAPTER 16

# Intelligence

*"The ability to observe without evaluating is
the highest form of intelligence."*
J. Krishnamurti*

*"The measure of intelligence is the ability to change."*
Albert Einstein

Now, we will bring mindful attention to intelligence as a factor in our quest to achieve our goals. The chapter emphasizes functional intelligence and the cognitive, physical, emotional, social, and spiritual intelligences that contribute to it.

According to *The Merriam-Webster Dictionary*, intelligence is *"the ability to learn or understand or to deal with new or trying situations; the ability to apply knowledge to manipulate one's environment or to think abstractly as measured by objective criteria (as tests)."* When you understand intelligence and how it links to behavior, performance, and relationships, you will be better able adapt to your situation as you identify, accept, and learn to work with your strengths and weaknesses.

## Multiple Intelligences

Howard Gardner, in the 1980s and 1990s, took us beyond thinking that intelligence was limited to IQ and reason. He identified multiple intelligences and defined intelligence as *"the capacity to solve problems or to fashion products that are valued in one or more cultural setting."*[25] Gardner pointed to the need to channel all the intelligences into functional performance.

While it is useful to separate the intelligences to better understand how we "work," they operate interactively. They are inseparable. The following five intelligences influence functional intelligence:

- Cognitive Intelligence
- Physical Intelligence
- Emotional Intelligence
- Social Intelligence
- Spiritual Intelligence[26]

The fifth, spiritual intelligence, is closely related to world view and wisdom. *(It will be described in the chapter on "Wisdom and Spiritual Intelligence—Knowledge beyond Intellect.")*

## Functional Intelligence

Functional intelligence is "the ability to act appropriately in an uncertain environment"[27] to achieve behavioral goals.

When any intelligence is diminished, functional intelligence is diminished. For example, a person with a high IQ who has little ability to deal with change or to communicate clearly and respectfully with people who disagree with them has a lower functional intelligence than one who is more accepting and in control of their emotions.

---

[25] Gardner, Howard, *Frames of Mind: The Theory of Multiple Intelligence*, New York: Basic Books, 1983/2003, p. 10.

[26] Di Filippo, Ivano, Di Filippo, Daniele, *Cognitive Readiness in Project Teams: Reducing Project Complexity and Increasing Success in . . . Project Management*, Routlege, 2021p. 87.

[27] J. Albus, 1991.

Functional intelligence is maintained and improved by using all the elements that contribute to mindful, conscious living: awareness, knowledge, wisdom, accepting, letting go, and continuously learning.

## Cognitive Intelligence

Cognitive intelligence is a general mental capability "that, among other things, involves the ability to reason, plan, solve problems, think abstractly, comprehend complex ideas, learn quickly, and learn from experience. It is not merely book learning, a narrow academic skill, or test-taking smarts. Rather, it reflects a broader and deeper capability for comprehending our surroundings—"catching on," "making sense" of things, or "figuring out" what to do."[28]

It is a measure of spatial, mathematical, and language abilities, memory and recall as well as motor skills, attention, perception, the ability to integrate multiple skills and perceptions, self-regulate, overcome biases, and make decisions.[29] Cognitive intelligence supports intellectual, occupational, financial, and environmental wellbeing.

## Physical Intelligence

Physical intelligence is concerned with the relationship between the body and mind, actively working to create better conditions for your body to thrive and ensuring you take steps to minimize stress and keep yourself healthy. *(See the chapter on "Working with the Body" for cultivating physical intelligence to support optimal living.)*

---

[28] "Mainstream Science on Intelligence," *The Wall Street Journal*, December 13, 1994.

[29] For a description of the elements of cognitive intelligence and IQ see https://blog.udemy.com/cognitive-assessment/

## Emotional and Social Intelligence

Emotional and social well-being rely on emotional intelligence (EI) to consider, understand, and manage your own emotions and recognize, and influence the emotions of others. EI enables healthy interpersonal relationships and stress management. Its focus is on being responsive rather than reactive. *(See the chapters on "Working on Emotions" and "Working in Relationships" for how EI is applied.)*

There are four dimensions of emotional intelligence.

- *Self-awareness* is to be aware of the presence of an emotion as a felt sense.
- *Self-management* is being responsive, thoughtfully acting in a situationally appropriate way.
- *Social awareness* is the ability to be aware of other people's emotions.
- *Social intelligence* is the ability to work with one's own and other people's emotions in relationships and one's environment.[30] Social awareness and self-management contribute to social intelligence.

Our emotional state affects our behavior, which affects those around us.

Social intelligence "is the capacity to play and work well with others. Or, put another way, it is the ability to develop relationships with other people and to handle social or public environments."[31] How well (or not) you are aware of how your words and actions may be received by others is the degree to which you display social intelligence. This aptitude is measured by how much you make the effort

---

[30] Boyatizis, Richard E., Goleman, Daniel, and McKee, Annie, *Primal Leadership: Realizing the Power of Emotional Intelligence*, Harvard Business School Publishing, 2001.

[31] Belack, Carl, et al, *Cognitive Readiness in Teams*, Routledge Taylor and Francis Group, 2019, p. 101.

to see yourself as others see you, to put yourself in their shoes and to act in a way that enhances mutual benefit. Emotional intelligence enables social intelligence with self-awareness and self-management.

EXERCISE
## Intelligence

We do not need scientific studies to understand and substantiate the importance of emotional and social intelligence. Look to your own firsthand experiences. Maybe you have met:

- the super "intelligent" person who views everyone else as idiots because they don't understand his explanation of the intricacies of some technology. This person doesn't realize that others don't necessarily want to know how it works; they just want to use it.
- a person with lots of potentially useful knowledge and experience who yells at people who disagree with him, calling them "incompetent imbeciles." Threatens. Verbally abuses.
- a bright, intelligent, knowledgeable person who is so shy that no one knows how smart they really are.

Reflect:

How do you feel when you catch yourself before your emotions take over vs. when you don't?

How does it feel when you are working with someone who listens, is empathetic, understands where you are coming from, synchronizes with you, presents him or herself in a suitable way for the situation, and shows concern for others?

How much more effective at achieving your highest goals are you when you present yourself in harmony with others and the environment, acknowledging your influence on and concern for them?

## CHAPTER 17

# Belief and Doubt

*"Your assumptions are your windows on the world.
Scrub them off every once in a while, or the light won't come in."*
Isaac Asimov

*"People like us who believe in physics, know the
distinction made between past, present, and future is
nothing more than a persistent, stubborn illusion."*
Albert Einstein

This chapter explores how beliefs affect the way we live and how we can use our intelligence to mindfully and open-mindedly question and change them to support wellness.

Any thought or concept you hold in your mind about the way things were, are, should be, or will be is a belief. Beliefs are thoughts we accept as being true. They affect our emotional state and behavior. And, any belief can be changed or discarded, if it is acknowledged to be a belief as opposed to a truth or fact.

Everyone makes predictions and assumptions and has biases. Assumptions become beliefs when you forget they are assumptions. Beliefs become biases when they are so strong or so buried in the subconscious that we cannot set them aside to focus on the facts.

Explore your own views, beliefs, and biases. Peter Senge advises us to turn "the mirror inward, learning to unearth our internal pictures of the world, to bring them to the surface and hold them rigorously to scrutiny," (to) ". . . carry on **'learningful' conversations** that balance inquiry and advocacy, where people expose their own thinking effectively and make that thinking open to the influence of others."[32]

## The Power of Beliefs

> *"When we blindly adopt a religion, a political system,*
> *a literary dogma, we become automatons.*
> *We cease to grow."*
> Anais Nin

The way you view the world influences your behavior. It is conditioned by personal, cultural, religious, and philosophical beliefs. *(The chapter on "Mental Models: Systems and Process Thinking" discusses views that support optimal living. They too are beliefs that must be questioned and validated.)*

If you believe you will fail at something, you are more likely to do so than if you believe you will succeed. If you believe you are floating in an ocean of love, you will be happier than if you believe you are adrift in an uncaring universe.

But beliefs can stand in our way. For example, Jim, the performance artist mentioned in the introduction, believes he is "nothing" unless he can dance. But he does not believe his prediction is a belief. He says it is his "reality."

If he recognized his "reality" was a belief, he could question and change it. He could choose to believe or predict that he could grow from any experience and direct his life going forward, so he could feel fulfilled no matter how unfortunate his injury was. Jim's belief

---

[32] Senge, Peter M., *The Fifth Discipline: The Art and Practice of the Learning Organization*, New York, NY: Currency Doubleday, 2006.

sets him up for worry, anxiety, depression, and panic. The alternative belief—"I will be able to handle whatever comes"—becomes a jumping-off point for positive action. It short circuits the worrying. It allows for hope.

Another person I know, a successful self-employed professional, often says, "Guaranteed, that won't happen." That belief keeps her from trying to make it happen or avoid it. It sets her up for disappointment when it does happen.

If Stephen Hawking had believed he was "nothing" unless he could live as he did before his ALS symptoms rendered him disabled, we would have lost the thinking and writing of a genius. Had Franklin Roosevelt given up on public speaking and politics when he could no longer walk, he would never have become president of the U.S.

## Question Everything

Are your beliefs adding value or standing in your way? Question even your most dearly held beliefs.

The Buddha advised his followers not to accept his teachings on blind faith, but to test them for themselves. In Judaism there is the concept of faith with reason. The word for "faith" in Hebrew means "knowledge." In Christianity, 1 John 4:1 says "Dear friends, do not believe every spirit, but test the spirits to see whether they are from God because many false prophets . . ."

But many people will fight to the death to hold to their beliefs because questioning them threatens stability. Heretics are burned at the stake. Books are banned. School curricula are altered to avoid confronting unpleasant facts. Conspiracy theories are taken as fact. Beliefs can provide a sense of certainty as a way of hiding from the truth.

If you don't think your belief is a belief, ask yourself how you know things are the way you think they are or will be. Exercise skillful doubt. Check facts and assess the source of your information. Question. Treat your beliefs as hypotheses.

To tell the difference between "God-sent" and "false spirits," try trusting in your inner felt sense. Continue to question and test until you are sure, convinced by your own experience. Then question some more to make sure you are not deluding yourself. *(The next chapter, "Mental Models," is about choosing assumptions, beliefs, and biases so they become tools for cultivating greater sustainable wellness. The chapter on "Devotion" describes the suspension of doubt and blind belief in devotional practice.)*

### EXERCISE
## Beliefs

The belief in God, and/or adherence to a religion, can be particularly difficult to reconcile with an open heart and mind.

Don't worry, we will not ask or answer the question, "Does God exist?" or if there is a soul that reincarnates or lives forever. And since we don't need to know the origin of it all to live well, we won't explore the fascinating subject of how and when our existence began. Instead, in this exercise we will look at these beliefs as examples of the questioning process.

**If you believe in God:**

What name and form does it/he/she/they take? How much is God involved with life, answering prayers, making miracles, and empowering prophets? What language does God understand? Does God possess a gender? Is there one or are there many? Is God an unknowable force that has no beginning or end? Is God only knowable as a felt sense or presence?

**If you don't believe in God:**

What makes you think there is no God? Could you ever know for sure? How do you explain what cannot be explained? What is the source of your belief?

Does your belief help you? Is it leading you to commit acts of kindness toward others, or to withhold kindness from some? Is it making you feel good about yourself or is it undermining your self-confidence and making you feel guilty? Is it providing a sense of comfort? How does it influence your relationships? Is it standing in the way of making good decisions?

CHAPTER 18

# Mental Models: Process and Systems Thinking

The chapter on belief and doubt stressed the importance of questioning your beliefs. This chapter explores mental models,* particularly **process,*** **systems,*** and **non-dual thinking.*** While these models are beliefs, they give us a way of looking at our universe and our place in it that closely aligns with the way things actually seem to be—impermanent, in motion, interconnected, in a chain of cause and effect.

The purpose here is not to persuade you to take on one of these models, but to set your mind to work to let go of any ideas that keep you from seeing things as they are.

Peter Senge defines mental models as "deeply ingrained assumptions, generalizations, or even pictures or images that influence how we understand the world and how we take action." The way you view the world influences your behavior, your values and goals, and the degree to which you can handle challenges like pleasure, success, pain, loss, unwanted change, and uncertainty.

Everyone has mental models. They are part of our mind's inner workings. Often these models are operating *below the line*, in the subconscious, out of consciousness. Mindfulness and skillful questioning allow you to bring your models to consciousness and *choose ones* that enable you to reach your goals because they accurately reflect the way things are.

## Systems Thinking

> *"At its broadest level, systems thinking encompasses a large and fairly amorphous body of methods, tools, and principles, all oriented to looking at the interrelatedness of forces, and seeing them as part of a common process."*[33]

The next chapter, "Mindful of Process," will focus on process and process thinking. Here the focus is on systems—sets of interacting people, places, things, and processes.

Systems thinking sees the universe as a system of intersecting systems within systems. For example, who we are as an individual is a system made up of endocrine, nervous, digestion, and other systems. These interact such that something happening in the nervous system can affect digestion and the other way around. Our individual system is part of family, organizational, geographical, and other systems. And these are part of planetary system, which is part of a solar system, within a galaxy, etc.

We can understand how central we are to our personal system and how that system is a speck dwelling on a much larger speck in the vast universe.

With systems thinking, we can look in on ourselves to make better sense of where we fit in our system of interacting physical conditions, interdependent people, places, things, relationships, concepts, values, policies, and actions. Then we can know what we are doing, why, where, and how we are doing it, and what impact it might have.

Systems thinking makes it clear there is uncertainty and that we are not in complete control. Any event kicks off a process that is influenced by and influences everything else in our complex of

---

[33] Senge, Peter M., *The Fifth Discipline: The Art and Practice of the Learning Organization*, New York, NY: Currency Doubleday, 2006.

systems. Because there are so many interacting factors, the effects of change are often delayed; results are difficult, if not impossible, to predict, and it is easy to lose track of the original cause.

For example, in a family system, a single act of infidelity or abuse can lead to divorce or separation with its wide-ranging effects on the children and their mental health, friendships, careers, finances, community, etc.

In an organization, making a change to the way sales are handled will cause a ripple effect through the organization's intersecting systems—accounting, manufacturing, fulfillment, administration—and externally in the lives of the salespeople whose compensation changes, affecting their families and community.

In society, changing values result in wide-ranging social and political impacts on elections, individual lives, and attitudes on things like climate change, abortion, immigration, and same-sex and interracial marriage.

## Worldview

> *"Truth is one. Paths are many."*
> Swami Satchidananda

Systems thinking is a worldview.* Like all views, it is imperfect, a tool used to gain a better understanding of how things really are. At some point, we need to "burn the boat," letting go into non-conceptual knowing.

Any model, whether Buddhist, Judeo-Christian-Islamic, Hindu, Animist, New Age, or one you weave together yourself, can work. But don't be fooled into dogmatic, rigid belief in a system that bills itself as the only way to salvation.

There is one Truth—reality. The closer you get to it, the more views and paths converge. If there are controversies, doubts, and heresies, the Truth has not been found, though open dialog is a way toward finding it. At some point, you know the model is a good one if it maps to reality and leads you to no longer needing it.

As said, a worldview model, like any belief system, is like a boat. It can be useful to transition from the shore of clinging to the shore of experiential living open to whatever comes. When you are ready, "burn the boat."

## Non-Duality

Non-duality is a worldview that goes back thousands of years. The fundamental idea is that there is an indescribable boundless whole within which life's movie is unfolding. We put concepts such as systems and process thinking around it to make it easier to live in the world.

Validation of this idea has emerged from neuroscientific studies[34] of the influences of social interaction on the brain. Personal validation comes through mindful, objective observation.

In the non-dual view, there is a unity of absolute and relative truths. Everything is appearing and dissolving in boundless space, as images appear in a mirror. The images are undeniably real, interdependent, impermanent, without solid substance.

The boundless space has many names—absolute ground, awareness, the ocean of love, and God, among others. The Buddha described the absolute ground symbolized by the mirror as a:

> "... sphere of being where there is no earth, no water, no fire, nor wind; no experience of infinity of space, of infinity of consciousness, of nothingness, or even of neither-perception-nor-non-perception; here there is neither this world nor another world, neither moon nor sun; this sphere of being I call neither

---

[34] Mills PJ, Barsotti TJ, Blackstone J, Chopra D, Josipovic Z., "Non-Dual Awareness and the Whole Person," Glob Adv Health Med., May 21, 2020, https://www.ncbi.nlm.nih.gov/pmc/articles/PMC7243377/

## MENTAL MODELS: PROCESS AND SYSTEMS THINKING

*a coming nor a going nor a staying still, neither a dying nor a reappearance; it has no basis, no evolution, and no support: it is the end of dukkha\*.*[35]*" (Ud 8.1)*[36]

The relative realm, the display of images, is the realm of things, of this and that, doing and not doing, me, you, and others. This is where your play is unfolding. It is what is happening in the mirror.

The absolute and relative are indivisible. You can't separate the images from the mirror.

*Thinking that the relative is all there is leads to unnecessary suffering.*

*Thinking that objects are solid and self-sustaining leads to unnecessary suffering.*

*Dismissing the relative as an illusion leads to unnecessary suffering.*

*Going beyond distinctions to both/and thinking eliminates unnecessary suffering.*

So what? When you take a non-dual view, it makes it clear that clinging, even to a solid sense of self, is futile. It helps you settle into a relaxed state of awareness while letting go into taking your roles and responsibilities "seriously."

An often-heard comment is that non-dual, systems-and-process thinking is uncomfortable and discouraging because it makes things seem out of control, so that doing anything is futile. In time, as the reality of being out of control in an ocean of open awareness becomes your reality, there is a letting go into the unfolding movie, playing

---

[35] *Dukkha* is a Pali word that is translated as suffering, dissatisfaction, stress, or unease. In Buddhism the end of *dukkha* is *nirvana*.

[36] Ajahn Amaro, "The Buddha on Non-Duality" http://tibetanbuddhist encyclopedia.com/en/index.php/The_Buddha_on_Non-Duality

your role in the relative realm, as best as you can, without attachment. In the non-dual view, the absolute and relative co-exist.

### EXERCISE
## Systems Thinking

What is your worldview? If you think you don't have one, think again. Maybe it is that there is no such thing and that chaos reigns. *(Check out the chapter on "Belief and Doubt.")*

Does your worldview match up with the reality you perceive? Does thinking about it make a difference?

How does the systems thinking perspective make you feel? Is it comforting? Is it realistic?

What is left when you erase all the system boundaries you have imagined?

How does conceiving of an absolute non-dual realm, in which everything is appearing as images in a mirror, make you feel?

CHAPTER 19

# Mindful of Process*

> *"If you can't describe what you are doing as a process, you don't know what you're doing."*
> W. Edwards Deming

Processes are the active elements of systems. This chapter focuses on how process thinking enhances our ability to better understand and manage our lives.

A process is a set of steps that creates an outcome, a result like a fresh coat of paint, a decision, or an emotional reaction. Process thinking says that every outcome is the result of a process. Everything is caused by something—thoughts, feelings, actions, and events under conditions such as cultural and personal beliefs and external circumstances.

## Inner Processes—Inner Workings

In the chapter on "Feelings and Perceptions," we saw the link between a direct experience, our feelings about it, and how they affect behavior. This link is an inner, often subconscious, process that directly affects the way we live.

Inner workings operate behind the scenes in the form of psychological, physical, emotional, and transpersonal* processes. These interact to drive observable behavior, operating either above or below the line. If they are above the line, you are conscious of them; if they are below the line, you are not. Either way, they are operating.

The more you sense and comprehend the processes that affect your life—everything from the way you do your work to the causes of your opinions, emotions, and behavior—the greater your ability to be responsive rather than reactive. Responsive, you can understand why you do what you do. You can moderate behavior and be better able to work with interruptions and distractions.

Inner processes are fast-moving chains of events cycling through:

- Direct contact (touching fire)
- Physical sensation (hot)
- Feeling (pleasant, unpleasant, or neutral)
- Reflection (labeling, analyzing, liking, disliking)
- Decision (clinging or letting go)
- Action (thinking, planning, saying, doing).

The process may happen so fast that you perceive it as a single step from contact to reaction. Mindfully conscious of inner workings, you can control your action.

For example, when someone is faced with a demand to do something quickly, the reaction may be excitement at the challenge or paralyzing fear at not being able to do it. The reaction results from the interplay among factors like insecurity, over or under estimation of personal skills, fear, anger, the environment, and technical skills. Conscious of the process, it is possible to note the urge to react and to respond instead.

## Distractions

Insight into processes helps in handling distractions. For example, when a lovely experience, like being immersed in the enjoyment of a beautiful piece of music, is interrupted by a noise, you may immediately drop back into the experience without being distracted. The interruption comes, you notice it, and pay it no mind. Or, you are so absorbed in the music that you don't even register the noise. Your enjoyment of the music is unfazed by the interruption.

Alternatively, you could find yourself distracted, lost in thoughts about the interruption. Mindful of that, you may be able to bring yourself back to the music. Unmindful, you are lost on a *mind trip* to who knows where.

Interruptions and distractions may be external or internal. External interruptions might be sounds, sights, smells, or physical sensations. Internal events are thoughts and feelings. Interruptions become distractions when you react to them.

Distractions take you out of direct experience into thinking. For example, looking for the source of the noise during the concert, thinking how great it would be to share the wonderful experience with a loved one, or worrying about whether you turned the water off at home all are distractions that take you away from the full experience of the music.

An event triggers a train of thought. The earlier in the train ride you become aware of the distraction, the easier it is to choose where to turn your attention so you can either step off the train and return to the music, or you can consciously continue the ride, choosing to stay on it or unable to step off.

Unaware of your process, you are just on the train, driven by events. You don't really know where you are going or how many interruptions will take you from the train you are on to another one. At some point you may wake up, remember the music, and return to listening or realize that you have been distracted and missed half the concert. If you are mindfully aware, whenever you wake up there is a moment of awareness to recognize and celebrate. Unmindful, waking up is just another interruption.

### EXERCISE
## Process Thinking

Think of an emotional reaction you have experienced—for example, becoming angry or happy about something.

What triggered the reaction?

What sequence of events took place in your mind from the trigger to the expression of your emotion?

What sensations and feelings were triggered? Were they triggered by thoughts? Did the thoughts trigger more thoughts and feelings?

Where in the chain of events could you have changed the outcome?

If you were aware of the process but unable to change it, were you accepting or frustrated?

How did your state of mind, worldview, and beliefs influence the process?

CHAPTER 20

# Wisdom and Spiritual Intelligence—Knowledge beyond Intellect

*"For all the subtlety of his teachings, the Buddha had a simple test for measuring wisdom. 'You're wise,' he said, 'to the extent that you can get yourself to do things you don't like doing but know will result in happiness, and to refrain from things you like doing but know will result in pain and harm.'"*[37]
Thanissaro Bhikku

Wisdom is deeply understanding the way things are and the intention to skillfully apply that understanding in life. Awareness, mindfulness, worldview, models, and beliefs contribute to wisdom.

This chapter weaves together spiritual intelligence and the understanding of wisdom that we have been working with. Wise understanding is realizing and accepting that things as they are—including uncertainty, imperfection, change, interdependence, and paradox—are unavoidable parts of life.

---

[37] Bhikkhu, Thanissaro, "The Integrity of Emptiness," AccesstoInsight.org, 2006. http://www.accesstoinsight.org/lib/authors/thanissaro/integrityofemptiness.html

With wisdom comes highly effective decision making and compassionate action. Your ability to accept, let go, and be content is the measure of your wisdom.

You strengthen your spiritual intelligence and attain wisdom by opening your mind, exploring your experience, questioning your beliefs, and accepting reality, even if you don't like it. *(See the chapters on "Belief and Doubt," "Mental Models," and "Process.")*

As previously noted, attachment, aversion, and ignorance cause the self-imposed stress that drains your energy and keeps you from living as best you can. Wisdom dissolves ignorance, the ultimate cause of attachment and aversion. Wisdom results in compassion for those (including oneself) who are unmindfully driven.

## Spiritual Intelligence

> *"Spiritual intelligence is the central and most fundamental of all the intelligences, because it becomes the source of guidance for the others.*[38]
> Stephen Covey

Spiritual intelligence is the "ability to behave with wisdom and compassion while maintaining inner and outer peace regardless of the circumstances."[39] Another definition has it as "the human capacity to ask questions about the ultimate meaning of life and the integrated relationship between us and the world in which we live. It results in an increase in psychological well-being."[40]

---

[38] Covey, Stephen. *The 8th Habit: From Effectiveness to Greatness*, Simon and Schuster: 2004, p. 53.

[39] Wigglesworth, Cindy, "Integral Theory and Its Relationship to Spiritual Intelligence," DeepChange.com, https://deepchange.com/IntegralSpiritualIntelligence2011.pdf.

[40] Abasi, Reza, Farahani, Hojjatollah, Sahebalzamani, Mohammad, and Talebi, Mehdi, "The Relationship between Spiritual Intelligence with Psychological Well-Being and Purpose in Life of Nurses," *Iranian Journal of*

Spiritual intelligence implies an experiential, practical, realistic, unbiased, objective perception of where we fit in the universe, our inner workings, our relationships, and how the system works. A realistic worldview validated through practice and experience contributes to spiritual intelligence.

Spiritual intelligence is not religion, though it is compatible with some parts of some religions. Like any intelligence, it can be cultivated to increase comfort with paradox, irrationality, setbacks, uncertainty, and continuous change.

Robert Emmons boils spiritual intelligence down to five capabilities:

1. Recognizing that there is more at work than our physical and conscious psychological states
2. Experience of heightened states of consciousness—states of bliss, out-of-body experiences, etc.
3. Seeing day-to-day experience as sacred
4. Using methods such as prayer, meditation, and contemplation to address problems
5. A tendency to be virtuous and oriented to the benefit of others as well as oneself.[41]

Danah Zohar, who coined the term "spiritual intelligence," identified 12 principles:

1. *Self-awareness*: Knowing one's own values and beliefs
2. *Vision and value led*: Basing action on principles
3. *Positive use of adversity*: Using adversity as a learning opportunity, being resilient

---

*Nursing and Midwifery Research,* Jan-Feb 2013, https://www.ncbi.nlm.nih.gov/pmc/articles/PMC3748553/

[41] Emmons, R.A., "Is Spirituality an Intelligence?" *The International Journal for the Psychology of Religion*. 10, 27–34.

4. *Holistic*: Seeing everything, including oneself, as part of a complex system of interacting people, places, and things
5. *Compassion*: Feeling what others feel as if you were feeling it; seeing them as no different than you. Wanting to help.
6. *Celebration of diversity*: Accepting and valuing diversity among people
7. *Field-independent*: Possessing, expressing, and defending one's own views in the face of resistance from others; self-assurance
8. *Asking fundamental "why" questions*: Needing to know why things are as they are
9. *Ability to reframe*: Assessing problems and issues in the context of the big picture
10. *Spontaneity*: Transcending beliefs and mental models, responsive to the needs of the moment
11. *Sense of vocation*: Desiring to be of value to others, to serve
12. *Humility*: Understanding and acknowledging accurately one's place as one player among many in the universe[42]

## Wise Understanding

> *"Wisdom tells me I am nothing.*
> *Love tells me I am everything.*
> *And between these two my life flows."*
> Nisargadatta Maharaj

Putting all the spiritual intelligence principles and capabilities together doesn't mean to memorize them and cultivate each one separately. It is once again about stepping back, to become increasingly self-aware, accepting, and letting go.

---

[42] Zohar, Danah, "Learn the Qs," https://danahzohar.com/learnqs/. Accessed April 20, 2023.

Nisargadata's words point to the paradox that we can recognize both that we are an everchanging, impermanent drop in a boundless universe *and* the presence of a self that lives and loves in the relative world. This is the message of self-awareness, systems, process, and non-dual thinking. It is the foundation for wellness and optimal performance.

Wisdom is knowing that:

- There is *mystery*—"more than meets the eye."
- Clinging*, needing things to be different than they can be, is stressful and causes suffering.
- Our relative world is appearing in boundless awareness in which things—including oneself—are interdependent, subject to change resulting from a chain of cause and effect, impermanent, and without solid substance.
- Mental models, constellations of concepts, filter our experience and can both help us navigate our world and stand in our way.

We can change our mental models and, with practice, go beyond concept to experience freedom.

## Wise Intention

Wise intention is to cultivate wise understanding and use it to live skillfully and ethically, to do no harm and, if you can, to contribute to your own well-being and the well-being of others.

Wise intention expresses itself in persistence, courage, resilience, empathy (understanding or feeling what others are experiencing), kindness (wishing well), compassion (the desire to avoid or alleviate suffering), and realistic expectations. These contribute to healthy relationships and the ability to make the best of anything that comes.

Do *not* expect a spontaneous permanent awakening (though it could happen). For most of us, wisdom, and the peace and power it brings, comes and goes. We fake it until we make it. There are moments when the light of wisdom dispels the darkness of ignorance. With wise intention, these moments become more frequent and longer lasting as you persistently change the conditioning, beliefs, habits, and models that stand in the way.

### EXERCISE

## Wisdom

In your own words, summarize wisdom and how awareness, beliefs, mental models, and spiritual intelligence contribute to it.

Are you committed to wise intention?

Each day for 30 days, read and repeat Nisargadatta Maharaj's mantra: *"Wisdom tells me I am nothing. Love tells me I am everything. And between these two my life flows."*

After each week, note how this understanding influences the way you feel and behave and any changes from week to week.

CHAPTER 21

# Recap: Relax, Observe, Allow, Do, Repeat

*"Enlightenment\* is an accident, but some activities make you accident prone."*
J. Krishnamurti

*". . . Seeking means to have a goal but finding means to be free, to be receptive, to have no goal."*
Hermann Hesse

The "Foundation," "Ideals," and "Mindset" sections present an overall model. There is much to think about. The Path is complex and yet there is a simplicity to it: become self-aware, accept what was and is, and let go into the future, allowing your skills, intelligence, and experience to flow.

This chapter is a recap of the basic concepts to summarize key points so you can apply them to the peaceful warrior's "work" to solve the problem of self-imposed stress. Solving that problem, you can relax to be more comfortable with yourself—content, calm, effectively active, and confident that you are ready for anything.

It takes effort to let go of habits, unfounded beliefs, and the need for certainty, and to instead cultivate a mindset that reflects reality and serves you well. That mindset is based on concepts to be digested over time, to transition from intellectual understanding to experiential knowledge.

While you may immediately and permanently experience perfect peace and freedom, it is more likely that you will experience moments of it. Experiment. See what happens when you take on the belief that you are operating from a calm center that opens to a boundless ocean of awareness in which all things are interconnected in an ongoing dance of change. The more you experience that calm center, the more your belief becomes reality.

---

*The Path is complex and yet there is a simplicity to it: become self-aware, accept what was and is, and let go into the future, allowing your skills, intelligence, and experience to flow.*

---

Wise understanding and effort bring glimpses of peace and freedom. Over time, the glimpses become longer and more frequent. The effort becomes easier and easier, until it becomes effortless.

Find the right balance—don't over-effort; don't under-effort. Both are symptoms of impatience and attachment. Let go and allow your skills and experience to influence skillful behavior.

## Core Concepts

Using mindfulness, intelligence, and a mindset influenced by systems, process, and non-dual thinking, the mind can open to both experience the vast boundless absolute nature of the universe *and* master life in the relative realm of relationships, social conditioning, jobs, religions, personal psychologies, and beliefs.

The problem, symptoms, causes, and solution are:

## RECAP: RELAX, OBSERVE, ALLOW, DO, REPEAT

- Self-imposed stress creates discomfort, dissatisfaction, and the dis-ease that blocks wellness.
- Symptoms are anxiety, anger, fatigue, depression, dissatisfaction, compulsions, obsessions, weakened immune system, physical tension, and being reactive as opposed to responsive. These result in relationship and work issues.
- The causes of self-imposed stress are attachment, aversion, and ignorance:
  - Attachment—clinging to what cannot be kept, needing things to be different than they can be
  - Aversion—clinging to the need to push away and deny what you feel is unpleasant
  - Ignorance—not accepting the reality of interdependence, inevitable change, uncertainty, a false sense of self, and that things will not always go as you'd like them to
- The solution is to cultivate sustainable wellness by changing your mind through courageously, patiently, and persistently questioning everything—including your most cherished beliefs and your sense of self—to eliminate the fear, attachments, habits, and mental models that stand in the way of living as best you can.

Sustainable wellness is attained through self-awareness, acceptance, and letting go:

- Learn to step back from the perception of a solid self to experience presence in a calm center that opens to vast, boundless, nameless awareness, the ocean of love, God, or whatever you choose to call the unnamable.

*"Stay in the center, and you will be ready to move in any direction."*
Alan W. Watts

> *"We come spinning out of nothingness, scattering stars,*
> *the stars form a circle . . . and in the center, we dance."*
> Rumi

- Cultivate and apply mindfulness to objectively observe and accept things as they are, confidently and courageously letting go into life's flow.
- Become comfortable with unease, paradox, uncertainty, change, and not being in control.
- Know that love is vital to our lives, both as a boundless unlimited, unconditional energy, and the emotion we experience and express in relationships with ourselves and others.
- Develop a realistic understanding of the way the world works, where we fit in it, and the way internal processes, inner workings, operate to change our perspective and perceptions, and influence feelings and behavior.
- Accept that while concepts and knowledge are useful, awareness and wisdom are non-conceptual, "in-your-bones" knowing.

> *"A sense of the universe, a sense of the all, the nostalgia which seizes us when confronted by nature, beauty, music—these seem to be an expectation and awareness of a Great Presence."*
> Pierre Teilhard de Chardin

- Realize that *the path is the goal.*

Concepts are interesting, useful, even inspiring, but it is when they are applied in practice that they become transformative. *(The next section, "Practices," gives you meditation and body awareness tools to apply to work with to cultivate the wellness that enables you to perform optimally at work and in community.)*

EXERCISE

## Recap

Write or record in your own words the basic takeaways from the first sections.

Review your summary from time to time to see if your understanding and perceptions have changed.

SECTION 4

# Practices

What is gained by study, analysis, and practice is transformed into living experience through practice.

*"If you do not put it into practice,
the teachings, like a great medicine held only in one's hand,
will not be able to nourish you back to health."*
Samadjirajasutra

*"This being human is a guest house.
Every morning a new arrival.
A joy, a depression, a meanness . . .
meet them at the door laughing,
and invite them in.
Be grateful for whoever comes,
because each has been sent
as a guide from beyond."*
Rumi

As a peaceful warrior, gratefully accept everything that comes your way as fuel for your effort to live as best you can.

This section is a collection of practices or techniques. Foundation practices cultivate mindfulness and concentration using concepts, sound, mind-revealing experiences, and body awareness. These enable working with pleasure, pain, and emotions in the day-to-day experiences of relationships, livelihood, and community. The same practices can lead to temporary and permanent relief from unnecessary stress.

## Make Everything Part of Your Path

The path is the goal. It is using what you have—your situation, emotions, mindset, body, breath, work, relationships—to continuously improve your capacity to be self-aware, to accept and let go so you can live well.

Some ask: if all we need to do is let go of all attachments and realize that it's all perfect here and now, what need is there for a process?

Letting go to spontaneously, without effort or path, realize awareness—free of all attachment, aversion, and ignorance—may be possible. But letting go is not easy for most of us. We need a way to go beyond the mental habits that keep us from "dropping into the river," as in the analogy of the person clinging to a branch on a riverbank in Chapter 3. So, we combine wisdom and method in a path that we make part of everyday life. Then, letting go happens naturally as wisdom dawns and life becomes the path.

## Beyond Easy Fixes

There is no step-by-step recipe or instruction. There are many programs, some with five, seven, eight, and nine steps. Some of them work. But only if the *steps* are woven together like the *strands* of a rope.

The path is non-linear and more like a woven rope or mosaic than a climb through stages of development. The basic strands—wisdom, meditation, skillful behavior—have been around for thousands of years, expressed in many ways through a variety of belief systems.

While easy-fix programs may be useful for a while, I suggest you go beyond promises of Nirvana, "heaven on earth," or perfect happiness. They can be traps that exchange one set of beliefs for another but never free you from beliefs.

SECTION 4: PRACTICES

You may find it helpful to blend religion, psychotherapy, a guru, New Age spirituality, ancient spiritual practices, stress-relief meditation and medication, diet, body work, faith, and anything else that helps. You can make them parts of your process, but don't think any one of them is going to save you.

Save *yourself* by becoming aware of yourself and your basic, peaceful clarity. Seek perfection but don't be attached to achieving it. Don't over-effort and don't under-effort. Be persistent and patient. Let wisdom unfold gradually as you drop away the things that stand in the way of experiencing it.

> "Enlightenment is an accident, but some
> activities make you accident prone."
> J. Krishnamurti

## Next Steps

The next steps are to go through the chapters in this section and apply the practices.

The first chapter, "Method," is a broad view of the use of concepts and techniques to achieve your goals. The next five chapters address meditation and body work. They set a foundation for working with pleasure and pain, the emotions, and mind-revealing experiences. And these set the foundation for working in relationships at work and in community.

As mentioned earlier, there is a lot to think about and to do in this book. The best approach is to take it slow and easy, allowing your mind to digest the concepts, choosing and using the techniques that fit into your lifestyle.

CHAPTER 22

# Method

*"Submit to a daily practice.*
*Your loyalty to that is a ring on the door.*
*Keep knocking, and the joy inside will eventually open a window,*
*and look out to see who's there."*
Rumi

This chapter provides a context for the following chapters which focus in on individual practices.

To receive the most out of the concepts, tools, and techniques you are reading about here, apply them and see if they work for you. Just knowing and thinking about them is not enough. That would be like reading a book and watching a video about how to swim but never jumping into the water.

Understand what the methods are meant to do: try them, tweak them, adapt them to your situation, and make them yours. Weave a personal wellness- and wisdom-based lifestyle.

Teachers and coaches are helpful to clarify, train, and give feedback—though, in the end, you become your own guru*. You become a midwife who brings forth your innate wisdom.

Some methods may be useful for a while and then, when they have served their purpose, they may be replaced by others. At times, you may stop using any techniques and simply rest in continuous awareness (but remember that it is easy to fall asleep and think you are awake). Apply the right level of persistent effort. Take it seriously AND play and have fun with it.

## Basic Approaches

"Yoga" means *union* or *oneness*. Yoga is more than an exercise program. It is a system of spiritual self-development for training the mind through self-observation, awareness, and letting go. While yoga is mostly associated with India, there are Tibetan, Japanese, and other versions. Its principles can be applied in any culture or context. In many ways martial arts and some exercise programs are forms of yoga.

In yogic tradition, there are five basic approaches to realizing peace and freedom. They are the ways of knowledge, devotion, skillful action in the world, the body, and meditation. These are woven together into an individual's path with one usually being predominant. All of them lead to the same result: freedom from anything that stands in the way of realizing calm, peaceful presence in action.

1. The **path of knowledge** uses the intellect to go beyond intellect. It explores and changes the way you view the world. It cuts through ignorance to reveal wisdom. It uses the concepts covered in the previous section.
2. The **way of devotion** dissolves any sense of separation with unconditional love. The devotee becomes one with a devotional object (e.g., God, the universal force, nature, humanity, a saint, or a guru) to go beyond attachment to realization.
3. The way of **skillful action** is the path of dedicated service. Every act is a devotional act dedicated to the effort to become free.
4. The way of **the body** uses the breath and physical exercise to cultivate health and explore the mind-body relationship, to go beyond "thinking about" to experiencing.

5. The way of **meditation** uses meditative processes to cultivate mindfulness and concentration, going beyond intellect to gain insight. As meditation practice matures the other approaches blend into a unified whole.

Your predominant approach fits your personality and its tendencies. Intellectuals will be drawn to the path of knowledge, which will free them to go beyond their intellect. Those more comfortable with physical sensations and felt sense will be drawn to the way of the body. Others will be drawn to devotion, the path of action, or meditation.

No matter which approaches you use, the end is the same—realizing oneness as the practitioner's basic nature. All approaches boil down to cultivating self-awareness, acceptance, and letting go to experience each moment objectively, in Flow.

## Right Where You Are

The path begins and ends right where you are. You don't have to drop out or change anything other than the mental models, beliefs, biases, and habits that stand in the way.

You can be "in the world but not of it." You don't have to live in silent isolation in a monastery, *ashram*,* or cave to become enlightened (though for some that may be the way). Right where you are, in the marketplace, you can live free of unnecessary suffering.

With practice you can see for yourself what is real and what is illusion or delusion. You can see for yourself what stands in the way and do something about it. You can act skillfully.

## Skillful Action

Skillful action includes the use of any or all concepts and techniques in a way that suits you and your goals. It is using everything that comes your way as fuel for burning away ignorance and clinging*.

In spiritual terms, skillful behavior boils down to refraining from harmful speech and action. But there are no absolutes. Circumstances and intention determine what is skillful and not skillful. For example, most ethical and religious traditions agree that killing or harming others is to be avoided. Yet each has a different definition of "others." To some, "others" are all beings, animals and humans alike. Some limit "others" to humans, or to members of the same family, tribe, race, religion, or country.

For example, there is the Buddhist story of Captain Great Compassion who killed a passenger on a ship to save 500 others. The captain acted out of compassion, even saving the one who planned to murder from the consequences of his act and saving the lives of the others. In the Middle Ages, Catholic priests blessed their crusaders and absolved them of the sin of killing.

Action is most skillful when it is informed by the values of kindness, compassion, and a sense of the interconnection between oneself, others, and your environment. Skillful action leaves no aftermath of guilt and remorse. Guilt and remorse become wake-up signals to renew the intention to act skillfully.

### EXERCISE
## Engaged Practice

Cultivate an engaged practice. Blend the concepts, tools, and techniques that you feel will enable you to experience a healthy, dynamic balance that emphasizes wellness.

Choose one method to begin with and work with it for, say, 40 days. See if you experience the benefits of ease of being, peace, calm, patience, contentment, and kindness. Be ready for the discomfort of confronting and changing unskillful beliefs and habits. Be aware of your resistance and self-criticism, and other thoughts and feelings that get in your way.

After reading through the whole section, I suggest you start with meditation and working with the body. They set a foundation for using the other methods. If you are more comfortable with one of the others, go for it. It doesn't matter as long as you keep stepping back, accepting, and letting go.

CHAPTER 23

# Training the Mind: Meditation

*"If the mind falls asleep, awaken it. Then if it starts wandering, make it quiet. If you reach the state where there is neither sleep nor movement of mind, stay still in that, the natural (real) state."*
Ramana Maharshi

*"Meditation will not carry you to another world, but it will reveal the most profound and awesome dimensions of the world in which you already live. Calmly contemplating these dimensions and bringing them into the service of compassion and kindness is the right way to make rapid gains in meditation as well as in life."*
Zen Master Hsing Yun

This chapter focuses on meditation as means for enhancing mindfulness and concentration. All the optimal living goals and concepts are about training the mind. They enable you to change your perspective, the way you view the world, so that you are able to cut through anything that stands in the way of wellness. *(The following chapters on "Meditation Practice" and "Body Work" will provide instruction for formal and informal practice techniques.)*

There are many meditation styles, including mindfulness or insight meditation, Transcendental Meditation, lovingkindness meditation, and more. They can help you to:

- Achieve freedom from self-imposed suffering

- Go beyond thinking to experience and wisdom
- Cultivate concentration (focus), mindfulness (attention), and awareness
- Gain clarity and insight to validate your goals and mental models
- Relax and relieve stress
- Elicit heightened states of awareness such as bliss, visions, lovingkindness, compassion, calm, and equanimity
- "Manifest" things, for example health, a new car, a happy relationship, or wealth

Here the emphasis is on meditation as a means for cultivating concentration (focus), mindfulness (attention), and awareness. These result in the clarity, insight, and stress relief needed to become free of self-imposed suffering and to be able to manifest what you want and be okay with what you receive.

## Be Careful

Be careful—like any method, meditation can be a trap.

Meditation master Namkhai Norbu Rinpoche pointed out that some meditators become addicted to blissful states of mind and use the techniques to avoid unpleasant feelings or just to manage stress without determining its causes. It is as if they planned a trip to Hawaii, arrived in California, and remained there in comfort without moving on. They never made it to Hawaii, their original goal.

There is a story of a highly skilled meditator, a yogi, who spent years in a cave, meditating. He reached the highest states of bliss with many special powers. When he finally left the cave to reenter the world, he was freaked out by the jostling and chaos of the marketplace.

Of course, "staying in California," or in the cave, may be enough for you, at least for the moment. But chances are the *calm abiding*\* you experience in your meditations will be interrupted by the invasion of disturbing emotions, thoughts, events, old age, sickness, and death.

Managing to be calmly responsive to these requires undistracted open awareness, and not only when you are meditating with your eyes closed in a quiet comfortable place. All the time.

## Cultivating Mindfulness and Concentration with Meditation

Meditation cultivates concentration and mindfulness—focus and attention.

According to Amisha Jha, a neuroscientist, there are three kinds of attention:

- Open attention—using a floodlight to see or be objectively aware of what is occurring in a broad expanse. This is mindfulness.
- Focused attention—shining a flashlight or laser to direct light on a chosen object. This is concentration.
- Executive attention—deciding what, within the field of open attention, to attend to and what to do about it, regulating responses with mindful awareness and discernment, avoiding distraction. This is the effort required to sustain open and focused attention.

Focused attention—concentration—elicits moments of silence, peace, and expansiveness beyond normal limitations. It cultivates calm abiding, the experience of simply resting comfortably in the present moment. Focused attention can lead to stress relief, healing, and even paranormal experiences and powers.

Open attention or mindfulness makes you aware of experiences and movement, telling you when you are distracted. It observes without judgment and enables insight into the nature of reality.

Together, concentration and mindfulness promote natural open awareness—the spontaneous experience of Flow and the optimal use of executive function.

Earlier chapters discussed "Mindfulness" and "Awareness" as concepts. Meditation brings these concepts to life.

## Meditation with and without Support

There are formal and informal practices. Informal meditation was introduced earlier with the Breather technique. If you are doing that during your day, you are already meditating.

Informal and formal practices share the same basic instruction: focus on an object, for example, the breath, the sensations of your body, or a sound, to calm your mind enough so you can observe your thoughts, feelings, physical sensations, and everything else that is occurring within and around you.

Using an object is called meditation with support. The support is an anchor you come back to in order to focus your attention. As the practice matures, concrete objects like the breath can be replaced by the felt sense of mindfulness itself—undistracted awareness and witnessing. This is called meditation without support.

It is easier to become "lost" or distracted when the point of reference is as subtle as awareness itself. So, you move between meditation with and without support until your mind naturally experiences undistracted awareness and Flow. As your practice matures, the awareness of being distracted becomes the signal to wake up and return to mindfulness.

Whether you are meditating with or without support, formally or informally, you experience *noticing, distraction, recognition, and returning*—undistracted noticing, becoming distracted, recognizing distraction, and returning to mindfulness.

Celebrate the moment of recognition. It is a moment of clear knowing. Everyone can become distracted. Not everyone recognizes it and returns to the point of attention. Returning increases the power of concentration. *(You may want to review the sub-sections on "Managing Distractions" and "Thought Trains" in the chapter on Mindfulness.)*

The more you practice, the less frequently you will get lost, and you will notice it more quickly when you do.

CHAPTER 24

# Exercise: Meditation Practice

*"Feelings come and go like clouds in a windy sky.
Conscious breathing is my anchor."*
Thich Nhat Hahn

This chapter provides instruction for formal and informal meditation techniques.

Treat meditation practice as you would any activity that promises to make you happier, healthier, and more effective. There are no hard and fast rules, except to relax, observe, and bring your attention back to your focal point whenever you become distracted. There will be thoughts and hindrances. Do not try to stop them; just observe them and be grateful you are mindful enough to notice them.

*Formal practice* is like going to the gym or a class, with a set-aside time and place. *Informal practice* on the other hand, is done moment to moment amid your normal activities. For example, during daily life, it can be remembering to return to mindfulness or an object like the breath, a healthy posture, a thought, or a sound. The Breather exercise introduced earlier is an example of informal meditation you can practice anytime. Informal practice includes making everything you do and experience an object of meditation.

### EXERCISE
## Formal Mindfulness Meditation Practice Instructions

Commit to a daily routine. Try it for 40 days. If you miss a day, don't worry about it; reset your intention, and start again. Consistency helps to strengthen your practice. If you think you cannot spare the time, you can trade a TV show for a session or wake up a few minutes early. But **don't make it a chore that creates more stress** in your busy life. If you are not ready to practice formally, just use the informal approach.

The meditation process is simple: *noticing, distraction, recognition, and returning*. But it is not easy. The untrained mind is often compared to a barrel of monkeys, flitting from one thought to another, reacting, and clinging. Training the monkey mind requires both effort and knowledge of internal processes. Meditation traditions identify five basic internal hindrances:

1. Sensory desire—attachment to what feels good
2. Feelings of hostility, resentment, and hatred
3. Half-hearted effort, laziness, lethargy, apathy
4. Restlessness and worry—obsessive thinking
5. Unskillful doubt, lack of trust in one's own ability

These hindrances are natural. They occur during both formal practice and in everyday life. When you recognize them, treat them as wake-up calls and bring your attention back to your meditation object or back to a calm, centered presence.

Formal practice is a means for cultivating a natural informal practice. Here are instructions for formal practice:

- Set aside a time of day that works for you.
- Set a timer. You can start with as little as five minutes, if that is all the time you feel comfortable with. Increase to a half hour as a goal. Stick with it for the full time you set, even if you are uncomfortable.
- Choose a quiet, comfortable spot where you are likely to be undisturbed and feel safe. If you can't find a perfect spot, no

## EXERCISE: MEDITATION PRACTICE

- worries, any place will do. In fact, some advanced meditators purposefully meditate in disturbing locations like cemeteries, jungles, and noisy marketplaces to hone their ability to be undistracted.
- You can practice in any posture—standing, sitting, lying down, or in motion. Sitting is the most common posture to start with. You can sit cross-legged on a cushion or seated in a chair. Sit comfortably erect.
- Minimize unnecessary movement—not like a statue, but comfortably relaxed and erect. *(If you find sitting quietly is a big challenge, you might want to start with the body awareness exercise in the chapter on "Exercises: Body and Breath Work.")*
- There is no need to subject yourself to pain and discomfort. However, there is benefit in being able to observe discomfort without reacting to it. For example, if you feel an itch, observe it without scratching it. Doing this strengthens self-confidence and concentration, though the most important thing is to relax.
- Become present by feeling the sensations of your body, the air against your skin, your weight against the chair or cushion.
- Choose a meditation object—the sensations of the breath, a sound, or a saying.
- Focus gently but firmly on your meditation object.
- Observe anything that comes up in or around you—thoughts, hindrances, distractions, feelings, judgment, external events, and your reactions to them. Observe the observing.
- Bring your attention back to your meditation object each time you notice you have become distracted.
- Be patient and do not expect any result. Just keep on practicing by noticing and coming back to your object.

## Informal—Moment-to-Moment—Practice

Formal practice prepares you for informal moment-to-moment practice in daily life by strengthening your powers of mindfulness and concentration and giving you the experience of calm abiding*.

The most important thing is to cultivate moment-to-moment practice, integrated into daily life so that everything becomes a meditation. Walking, you observe walking and the flow of thoughts and feelings and just walk. Doing the dishes, you observe doing the dishes, notice distractions, and just do the dishes. No matter where you are, you remember presence and awareness. Doing this leads to non-meditation, the complete integration of mindful awareness into your life.

Use mini-meditation breaks, like the practice of simply coming back to the sensations of your breath and body. You can set an alarm to remind you to take a break during the day. As your practice matures, you will recognizewhen you are reacting, tense, or uneasy and be triggered to STOP and take a break. You can take a mini-meditation break at a meeting, at a party, in the middle of a conversation, anywhere, anytime. When others are involved, keep it short, a second or two and they'll never know what you are doing. It is just a little pause.

Other methods in the subsequent chapters integrate meditation into daily life with focus on the body, relationships, the experiences of emotions, pleasure, and pain.

As with any exercise program, if you don't practice you won't get results. Take the 40-Day Challenge: practice formal meditation for at least five minutes a day and practice informal mindfulness for 40 days. See what happens.

Relax and enjoy.

___

CHAPTER 25

# Body Work

*"But if one observes, one will see that the body has its own intelligence; it requires a great deal of intelligence to observe the intelligence of the body."*
J. Krishnamurti

Every activity involves the body. Listen to and take care of your body and you will be better able to navigate through your life with dynamic balance, strength, and resilience.

This chapter and the one following provide understandings and techniques you can use as part of any formal and informal practices to promote well-being.

On the surface, bodywork means getting enough of the right kind of exercise and eating well. On a more subtle level, body awareness is a mindfulness meditation used to increase self-awareness and manage your stress and emotions by being in touch with physical sensations throughout the body—the breath, digestion, muscle tension, relaxation, your posture, etc.

Over time, you will become familiar with the sensations, the felt sense, of your feelings. You will get to know what it feels like to be calm and at peace resting in your body and what discomfort feels like. You will recognize the connection between your thoughts, feelings, and the felt sense of the body.

For example, unaware of an urge, one simply reacts to fulfill the urge. With body awareness, there can be choice; the urge is still there but it has become an object of mindfulness. You observe the physical sensations of deeply wanting or not wanting something. You may not be able to do anything but fulfill the urge. Mindful, set the intention to observe and not react to that urge, particularly if it keeps coming back to disturb your peace.

On the most subtle level, there is awareness of *energy* or *life force*. It is about the experience of the subtle body and the energy that flows through it. While not yet scientifically verified, thousands of years of yogic tradition, acupuncture, and ayurvedic medicine, along with contemporary personal experience, point to the presence of a subtle life force energy, called *prana* or *chi*, and a network of channels and centers through which the energy moves.

We will not go into this third level of bodywork beyond this brief mention. If you are interested in exploring further, you will want to look into yogic, Chi Kung, and other systems providing the techniques and concepts that enable you to perceive and work with the subtle energy. As always, choose teachers and teachings wisely. Rely on teachers with personal experience and a foundation in proven approaches.

## Body Awareness—Listen to the Body

In life, you are likely to experience physical damage, disease, and decay. You may be born into a physically challenged body. No matter what your condition may be, the goal of body work is to use the felt sense of the body and its sensations as a form of meditation and to cultivate healthy posture, movement, diet, and exercise to *relax* in your body even when your body doesn't feel good.

Body awareness is a form of meditation and a foundation for personal well-being. The body influences (and is influenced by) the mind, our posture, environment, health, where we place our attention, and mindset. Feelings, physical conditions, and stress surface as physical sensations. Tuning into them brings you mindfully to the present moment, aware of yourself and your surroundings.

To listen to your body is to be mindfully aware. Each change in sensations sends a message about physical and emotional well-being. When aware of a feeling of discomfort or pleasure, decide whether to observe it and let it pass. Take a moment to adjust your posture, take a hot bath, see a doctor, or be happy with it.

In many meditation techniques, the first step is to "drop into the body." It means to bring your attention to the felt sense of your physical sensations—the pressure of your weight against the ground or chair, the air against your skin, feelings, the sensations of the breath, tastes, smells, images, and textures. No matter where you are or what you are doing, dropping into your body brings your attention to the present moment, to the calm center, to natural mindfulness. Experience the felt sense of the body without thinking about it.

## Working with What You Eat and Drink

Any book on wellness and optimal living must address the way we use our eating and drinking to increase physical well-being, manage emotions, and cultivate mindful awareness.

There are two dimensions to consider when working with eating. One dimension is finding a diet that sustains physical health and suits your lifestyle. Skillful eating is about maintaining a healthy body—balancing physical activity, nutrition, sleep, relaxation, and immune support.

The mix of food and drink that keeps you healthy depends on your condition. One size does not fit all. With input from medical and nutrition experts and mindful of how you feel when and after you eat and drink, of your weight and general health, craft a diet that works for you. But be careful, because there is the other dimension to eating and it can lead you into obsessing about your diet.

*Hungry ghosts have large, empty bellies and skinny throats and tiny mouths.*
*They can never take in enough to fill their emptiness.*
*They suffer constant hunger and thirst.*

If eating were only about nutrition, life would be easy. But we experience emotional eating and eating for pleasure. We eat with our senses, looking and listening to take in what we need to fill ourselves. Emotional eating and eating for pleasure cause health issues like obesity, diabetes, and heart disease. *(The chapters on "Making the Best of Pain," "Enjoying Pleasure," and "Working with Emotions" are about how you can refrain from reactive behavior like eating and drinking to avoid pain and cling to pleasure.)*

## EXERCISE
## Mindful Eating

This exercise brings mindfulness to eating. You can do it anytime, either formally as a meditation or informally as a way of using your eating (as well as your drinking and smoking) to bring conscious awareness to daily life.

The formal practice is to bring attention to every step of the eating process while experiencing sensations, feelings, and thoughts:

- Intending to take a mouthful of food
- Taking the piece onto the spoon, fork, or chopsticks
- Bringing it to the mouth
- Placing it into the mouth
- Experiencing tasting, salivating, and feelings
- Chewing (you can count the number of chews)
- Swallowing
- Going for the next forkful.

The informal practice is to simply be mindful of the way you behave and feel when eating. The message here is to enjoy the pleasures of eating and drinking without clinging while being mindful of your physical and emotional well-being. An occasional ice cream binge, smoke, or drink to soothe your troubled mind is okay, but don't let it become a regular habit.

## Working with the Breath

Working with the breath is part of working with the body. The breath is the link between your mind and body. It is what connects you to your environment, the bridge to your life force.

Mindfulness of the breath brings insight and concentration. Breath control methods relax, energize, and heal the body. Inhalation brings in oxygen, invigorating the body. Exhalation releases carbon dioxide; it cleanses, relaxes, and heals the body.

Become familiar with the way your mind, body, and breath interact. Do you hold your breath when you are stressed or in pain? Does your breath speed up when you are anxious and slow down and deepen when you are calm? How do you normally breathe: shallow inhalations and exhalations, or full breaths, using your full lung capacity? Through the mouth or nose?

## Next Steps

To go from concept to experience requires practice. There are many—thousands or more—techniques to cultivate body and breath awareness, to promote health and vitality and maximize wellness and energy.

Breath and posture exercises cultivate both physical health and awareness. The systems I have found effective are *hatha* and *kundalini* yoga, swimming, Chi Kung, and Tai Chi. Dance, martial arts, and other movement systems are other options.

Experiment and find a system you are comfortable (but not too comfortable) with. If you have become too comfortable, you may be avoiding the work to overcome unhealthy posture and habits. Take a balanced approach that gently pushes the edge, letting go of unnecessary tension as the body adjusts to a healthy posture and Flow.

Regardless of the system you choose or the program you have pieced together, benefits come when you integrate body work into your daily life with the intention to develop a healthy body and mind. For example, standing and waiting, you can mindlessly slouch, get lost in fantasy, or fidget. Or, you can use the opportunity to *play* with your posture, breath, and mindfulness. Take a breather anytime, anywhere.

The next chapter explores working with your posture and breath so you can integrate body work into your formal and informal wellness practices.

CHAPTER 26

# Exercises: Body and Breath Work

*"Don't make the body do what the spirit does best,
and don't put a big load on the spirit that the body could easily carry."*
Rumi

This chapter contains exercises you can practice to make body awareness an integral part of your path. Be patient. Years or decades of habit, injury, disease, and poor diet make it a challenge to breathe, move, stand, and sit comfortably and healthfully. Apply skillful effort. Accept and let go.

## EXERCISE

### Breath Awareness and Diaphragmatic Breathing

The purpose of this exercise is to teach the technique of diaphragmatic breathing to promote breath awareness and deeper breathing.

It is generally more healthful to breathe through your nose. If that is not possible for you, investigate the cause and, if you can, correct it. In the meantime, breathe through your mouth.

Diaphragmatic, belly, or three-part breathing trains the body to make more effective use of the breath.

Relax. If you are straining, you are working too hard. The depth of your breath, the degree to which you fill your lungs, will change;

just breathe in until your lungs are comfortably full and breathe out without pushing.

You can practice this as a formal meditation and informally as part of your daily activity.

- Place one hand on your lower abs, below the navel, and the other on your chest.
- As you inhale, imagine letting your lower abdomen fill. The belly pushes gently into your hand and makes room for the diaphragm to drop down.
- Let the ribs expand and the air fill the lower part of your lungs
- Let the air continue to fill your lungs as your upper chest expands and the shoulders relax.
- Feel your chest expand into your hand.
- Sense the body becoming invigorated.
- Exhale—compress your belly bringing your diaphragm in and up. Compress your ribs and chest.
- Feel the body relaxing.
- Continue breathing this way: gently but with a conscious effort to fill and empty your lungs without straining.
- Let the steps blend into one another so your breathing is a continuous movement—like a flowing river, as it goes from nose to throat, down to the chest, the diaphragm, and deep into the belly. And on the exhale, let it slowly flow up and out.

You can add a visualization to this exercise:

> Imagine yourself by the ocean, breathing with the rhythm of the waves. Feel the breath as ocean waves of light and energy flowing through your body. Breathing in, your whole body expands and fills with light and energy. Exhaling, your body expels toxins and negativity. The waves of the breath touch every cell.

Remember—don't strain. Just sense your constraints and relax.

If you feel yourself getting lost in anxiety, take some relaxed, deep inhalations and exhalations to bring your attention to your body, and to calm down.

If you want more energy, breathe deeply and more forcefully to charge yourself up.

Count your breaths, from one to 10 and then back to one (if you lose your place, just start over) to strengthen concentration and relax the mind.

*(Note: Pranayama* (the yogic methods for using the breath), is beyond the scope of this book, but it is a very powerful set of practices. So be careful. You can find a starting point for exploring breath work on the internet, but make sure you are aligning with teachers and teachings that are authentic and work for you.)

---

## Posture

This exercise can be paired with the breathing exercise. It is a training in relearning a healthful posture.

Posture is a foundation for a healthy body. A relaxed and erect posture is invigorating. It wakes you up, relieves unnecessary strain, and allows your breath and inner energy to flow freely, to naturally heal and fuel your body and mind. Posture awareness is meditation in action.

Yoga's Mountain Pose and Chi Kung's *Wu Chi* posture are foundation postures. They can be practiced anytime, anywhere, for as long as you want. Instructions are below.

If you do nothing more than practice this posture, you will experience a greater sense of grounded stability with the readiness for dynamically balanced movement.

However, it takes work. You may experience discomfort when changing ingrained posture habits like slouching, hunching your back, rolling your shoulders forward and caving your chest, leaning to one side, and more. Poor posture may be comfortable because you are used to it or are using it to mask pain in your body. Correcting it is worth it in the long run. Owning up to and accepting the pain your old posture is hiding constitutes a step toward healing.

In the process, be kind to your body and patient. Learn the difference between healthy discomfort and harmful pain. Be persistent, gentle, and firm.

Try the exercise below for a minute or less and increase the time until being comfortably erect becomes natural. The exercise is both physical and a mindfulness meditation, with the object of attention being the sensations of the body. Commit to doing it every day as a formal meditation and informally during the day whenever you think of it.

## EXERCISE
## **Being Comfortably Erect**

Being comfortably erect is not a rigid, military-style attention. To the degree that you can, release unnecessary tension. Take a few breaths and relax. Let go. Drop your attention into your body.

If your physical condition does not permit this kind of posture, it is okay. Visualize or imagine the posture and let your physical body come into it as best it can. The attention and the intention are enough to change the way your energy is flowing and your mood. Be kind to your body. Guide it and let the body take the posture; don't force it.

While standing, take the following posture: [43]

- Place feet flat on the floor, shoulder width apart, knees slightly bent.
- Imagine a string gently lifting you from the crown of your head.
- Slightly tuck your chin to straighten the neck (the back of your head should be pulled gently back).
- Relax your head, neck, and shoulders.
- Make sure your tongue is resting comfortably, touching the upper palate just behind the teeth.

---

[43] Dye, Pam, "Wuji (Wu Chi)—Always," ForeverTaiChi.com, February 9, 2017, http://forevertaichi.com/2017/02/09/wuji-wu-chi-always/

## EXERCISES: BODY AND BREATH WORK

- Gently stretch the spine to align the centers of the head, chest, and lower abdomen.
- Gently roll your shoulders back and down, with your arms hanging at your sides and your hands open, fingers relaxed and comfortable.
- Let the chest lift and the mid back become active as the shoulders relax.
- Relax the lower abdomen, hips, and pelvis.
- Tuck your tail bone gently forward.
- Let the weight of your body fall through the hips to the thighs, behind the unlocked knees, ankles, and through the center of the feet.
- Feel your toes against the ground.
- Breathe naturally.
- Bring your attention to the space between your navel and pelvis.
- Allow your body to adjust itself into a comfortably erect posture, relaxed and energized.
- If you feel yourself slipping out of the posture, adjust and continue.

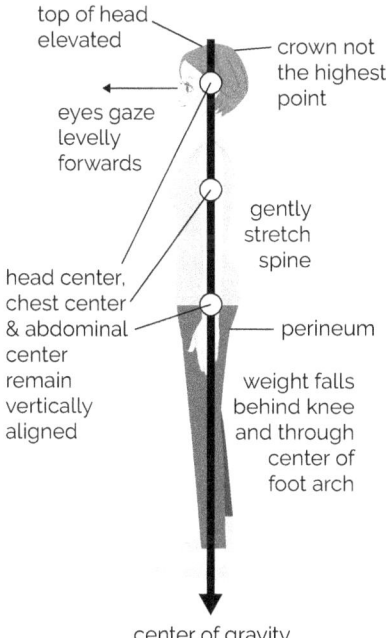

center of gravity

You can do a similar practice while sitting or lying down. The idea is to maintain a posture that is as healthfully relaxed and erect as possible while you are aware of the changing sensations of your body.

Practice body and breath awareness all the time. Whether you are sitting, standing, or walking, notice your posture and your breath. Just noticing will bring you back to the present moment. Then you can choose to adjust your posture to be alert, energized, strong, balanced, and ready.

---

CHAPTER 27

# Working with Sound

*"What makes us feel drawn to music is that our whole being is music: our mind and body, the nature in which we live, the nature which has made us, all that is beneath and around us, it is all music."*
Hazrat Inyat Khan

Sound is a powerful tool for cultivating concentration, calm, and healing. This chapter offers an introduction to the way sound and music tune your mind and body with hearing, listening, and making sound.

Sound has been used for thousands of years as a wellness technique. Sound vibration elicits an opening, a felt sense beyond normal perception. The sound of a gong, a chant, or music, even the sound of silence, is beyond concept.

Depending on your mindset, the setting, and the sound itself, sound can stir your heart, open your mind, relax, heal, or excite you. It can be used to build concentration and elicit "spiritual experiences" like trance states and expansion of normal perceptions. It can also annoy you, making you uncomfortable, anxious, and stressed; think of the sound of metal scraping against glass, the sounds of whining, anger, or chalk screeching on a blackboard (if you remember blackboards and chalk).

Your perception of sound depends on your mindset and setting:

Imagine music is playing. It's a playlist you like, one that gets you up and dancing. But you are trying to go to sleep after a long, grueling day and the music is coming from a neighbor's sound system. Chances are you won't feel like dancing. You might toss and turn, seething in annoyance.

Imagine the same music at a party. If you let it, it takes over your body and mind and you are immersed in movement. You find Flow in the dance.

## Hearing, Listening, Observing, Feeling

Sound is a vibration that moves through space as an acoustic wave. Hearing is the passive perceiving of sound. Listening is to intentionally give your attention to a sound. It is actively trying to comprehend what you hear. Expanding on that definition, active listening includes paying attention to what you perceive with all your senses. Sign language and body language are targets of active listening, even though there is no sound involved.

But working with sound goes beyond hearing and listening. Chanting, spiritual music, and sound healing tune the mind, heart, and body. The sound itself elicits an opening, a felt sense beyond normal perception.

For example, sound healing addresses issues like immune response, stress, anxiety, chronic pain, and depression. The use of sound for healing goes back thousands of years. The ancient Greeks believed that diseases can be cured using song and music. Plato and Aristotle linked music to the emotions. Mantras* have been used for centuries to cure disease and promote health and healing.

A 2012 study tasked two groups to spend 12 minutes each day for eight weeks using sound. One listened to relaxing music. The other practiced *kirtan kriya*, a meditative technique that involves chanting mantra*.

> *"At the end of the study the group that listened to relaxing music felt good, with 31.2% reporting substantial improvement in depressive symptoms and 19% scoring higher on a mental health survey. But the chanting group felt better, with 65.2% reporting fewer depressive symptoms and 52% reporting better mental health scores."*[44]

## Making Sounds: Chanting and Mantra

When you sing, chant, or play an instrument, it has a deeper effect than if you simply hear and listen. Singing, for example, is said to produce benefits such as stress reduction, pain relief, and improving lung function. Through rhythmic drumming, singing, and chanting, you can experience extraordinary trance states.

Chanting is a meditative practice that engages the breath, vibrates the body, and allows the mind to relax and open. It is the rhythmic reading of scriptures or prayers or repetition of sounds, words, or phrases. Chanting practices use mantras to cultivate concentration and to elicit specific results.

Mantras are sounds or phrases that may be chanted out loud or silently. The word is from Sanskrit: *man* means "to think" and *tra* "to liberate." A mantra is a thought or sound that liberates or clears the mind.

If you want to steady the mind and cultivate greater concentration, the mantra can simply be a meaningless sound you use as the object of your meditation. But if you want to use mantra for

---

[44] (This article is one of many that point to the effectiveness of sound in healing. It refers to scientific studies.) Purtill, Corinne, "Turns Out "Sound Healing" Can Be Actually, Well, Healing," *Quartz*, January 20, 2016, https://qz.com/595315/turns-out-sound-healing-can-be-actually-well-healing/#:~:text=Sound%20healing%20adherents%20say%20that,%2C%20sleep%20disorders%2C%20and%20PTSD.

transformation, there are specific sounds and phrases recommended to elicit specific states including peace, healing, clarity, strength, financial well-being, attracting a partner, and freedom from unnecessary stress.

These sounds and phrases need not be from any particular tradition; any meaningful affirmation or sound you invest with power can be used. Though why not use mantras, sayings, or prayers that have been used for centuries for specific purposes? For example, *AHHH* is the ancient mantra of deep relaxation and letting go. That being said, any prayer or affirmation can be used.

As with any meditative technique, you can only really get results through experience. Choose a mantra, learn or give it meaning and intention, practice it for a while (say, 40 days), let go of unskillful doubt, and see what happens. Whether what happens is a placebo effect or not doesn't much matter if the effect is felt.

Set your intention, let go, and do the mantra until the mantra is doing you.

I encourage you to check out Lily Cushman's book, *A Little Bit of Mantras*[45] for an introduction to sacred sounds. There are many mantra videos and recordings available on the web. Explore a little and see what else you might find that appeals to your own personal tastes and interests.

## Spiritual Music

> *"Music is the mediator between the spiritual and the sensual life"*
> Ludwig Van Beethoven

Spiritual music is another dimension of sound that has the power to connect the singer and listener to the divine. This kind of music exists in the forms of spirituals, *kirtan* (Hindu chanting), hymns,

---

[45] Cushman, Lily, *A Little Bit of Mantras*, Sterling Ethos, New York, 2019.

and other forms of music. It can touch your soul, bring you to tears, or make you angry or happy. Or, it might make you want to dance!

Find a genre of music that bypasses your intellectual filters. It can be a song like "Amazing Grace," Carl Orff's "Carmina Burana," John Lennon's "Imagine," "Ave Maria," Gregorian chants, the Grateful Dead, or your national anthem. If it takes you out of your head and opens your heart, it is spiritual music.

### EXERCISE
## Meditation Technique—Experiencing Sound

In this exercise, experience and observe the felt sense of silence.

- Get comfortable and feel the sensations your body and breath.
- Follow your breath for a few minutes to calm your mind.
- Observe sounds.
- Be aware of whether you are listening or just hearing.
- Let go of listening and simply observe the sounds.
- As distractions take your attention, bring the mind back to hearing.
- Notice the silent spaciousness that sounds emerge in and dissolve into.
- Let go of observing and just be aware of hearing.
- Rest there.

Do you try to avoid silence, or do you seek it? Is it pleasant, unpleasant, or neutral? What do you feel when you are silent? What do you feel when you are immersed in sound?

Are you reactive or responsive? Are you aware of the difference between hearing and listening?

Observe what happens to your attention when you hear a sound: the hearing, the felt sense of the sound in your body, the shift into labeling it and thinking about it, and the beginning and end of the sound.

CHAPTER 28

# Make the Best of Pain: Open, Act, and Learn to Avoid Suffering

*"Experiences of pleasure and pain are inevitable. Suffering is optional.
If you can see and learn about thoughts, feelings, and body sensations—
and how they are related—
then you will be ready for pain when it comes. And it will.
Your practice is to watch and learn about these connections."*
Sayadaw U Tejaniya

*"The best way out is always through."*
Robert Frost

Pleasure and pain are both part of our reality, and each, handled skillfully, is an experience that can fuel happy, healthy, effective living. Pleasure and pain are doorways to either freedom or to dissatisfaction and suffering. You get to choose.

This chapter acknowledges the reality that pain is an inescapable part of life, separates pain from suffering, and offers an approach to skillfully work with it by stepping back, accepting, and letting go.

We have addressed the sense of being aware of the self as a process without a solid identity. When we step back and consider pain as an object of mindfulness, it becomes an interesting phenomenon. Not my pain, just pain. When it is not my pain, it loses its impact.

## Pain

If you have a body, you will experience physical pain. So, you might as well make clever use of it. With the right attitude, you can avoid unnecessary suffering and be better able to help yourself and be there for others.

Pain is a felt sense. It hurts. It may be the sensation of burning, stabbing, shooting, or aching. It may be dull, sharp, or nagging. My heart aches when I see the pain of people torn from their homes or suffering the loss of loved ones. My shoulder and hip hurt from old injuries and arthritis. My friend hates his job. Someone else is reliving painful past experiences. Anxiety, sadness, and anger are painful. Pinched nerves are painful. Mental suffering is painful. Eating too much ice cream is painful. Not being able to keep pleasure is painful.

Pain may be chronic or acute. It is an alarm signaling that something is wrong. Feel no pain and you are less able to protect yourself. Pain can be an opportunity to open, act, and learn. It can also knock you out into unconscious reactivity—panic, fighting, fleeing, overmedicating, suppressing, shutting down, freezing, denying, ignoring.

## What Doesn't Kill You Makes You Stronger

Your attitude toward pain makes the difference between effective response and reactivity. If your attitude is that pain is bad and unacceptable, you suffer unnecessarily. If your attitude is, *If it doesn't kill you, it will make you stronger,* that pain and painful situations are opportunities to fuel your work on yourself—then you *will* become stronger, more resilient, and better able to live as best you can.

There is a story that brings out the attitude of accepting pain:

> *"When a famous English scientist, Alfred Wallace, was a child, he came upon a butterfly struggling to get out of its cocoon.*

> *Seeing this was so sad and distressing, he gently tore open the tip of the cocoon. When the boy did this, the butterfly emerged from its cocoon easily, and the boy breathed a sigh of relief.*
>
> *The butterfly looked like it would now fly away. However, it was unable to spread its wings properly and ended up dying after weakly flapping them a few times. Alfred realized that the hard struggle to break out of the cocoon makes the butterfly strong; the butterfly gains the strength to maintain its life only by going through this painful process.*[46]

The butterfly was not complaining. It was doing what came naturally. Wallace projected his feelings about pain and struggle and acted in a way that killed the butterfly he sought to help. Conscious of our aversion to pain, we can use painful experiences to become strong enough to fly free.

## Opening and Accepting

Opening and accepting pain to fully experience it is skillful, though it seems counter intuitive and is difficult.

Opening and accepting allows for responsiveness. Skillful response may be the use of medication or other pain relief techniques to manage the pain or to apply other means.

I learned about opening and accepting when my friend Herb taught me how to stay warm on a freezing day. The cold was painful, and I was trying to fight it off—hunched over, tight, shoulders pulled together and rolled forward to create a circle around my chest. Herb's advice was to straighten up, accept the pain, and relax. "Let the cold in and let your body find its balance," he told me.

---

[46] Lee, Ilchi, *"Pain Can Give Us Wings,"* IlchiLee.com, May 19, 2022, https://www.ilchi.com/pain-can-give-us-wings/

Trying to avoid unavoidable pain creates tension that makes the pain worse. Suppressing pain drives it in rather than driving it away. Driven in, it will reemerge as post-traumatic stress, illness, muscle tension, and unproductive fear.

## Suffering

In our context, there is a difference between pain and suffering. Pain is an uncomfortable physical sensation caused by illness or physical or emotional injury.

Sadness and grief, for example, are painful. They morph into suffering when they settle in and become depression or anger. The pain of a pinched nerve morphs into chronic pain and suffering when it is ignored or compensated for by poorly adjusting posture or overmedicating.

Suffering is a long-lasting, self-imposed form of pain. It is the experience of distress, anger, misery, and depression, fed by the mind in reaction to pain. Your thoughts, beliefs, memories, and emotional reactions create suffering. Suffering is avoidable.

For example, barefoot, Jules steps on a tack; there is pain. Jules complains, "There shouldn't be tacks on the floor!" "Who put that tack there?" Or, "Why is it always me who finds tacks to step on?" "Will I get some disease from the tack?" In a rage, Jules might attack the person responsible for the tack.

Then, someone soothes the foot and diverts Jules' attention, and the pain is gone. Jules' reaction—everything following the initial pain sensation until letting the pain go—is suffering. Wanting things to be different than they can be is suffering.

## Chronic Pain

Chronic pain is a special kind of pain. While the pain of stepping on a tack lasts for a few seconds and minutes, chronic pain lasts for weeks, months, or longer. It may be the result of an injury, illnesses such as arthritis and cancer, pinched nerves, or other conditions.

Don't confuse chronic suffering with chronic pain. With chronic physical pain, it is easy to get caught up in thoughts like, *I can't live with this!* and, *Will it ever go away?* These thoughts lead to the mental suffering of chronic psychological states like despair, anger, and unrelenting grief. Using mindfulness and self-awareness, you can step back, accept, and let go.

While it is hard to accept chronic pain, applying the courage and wisdom to accept it avoids chronic suffering.

## Intense Pain

It is one thing to write and think about pain and quite another to experience it or watch a loved one experiencing it. A friend told me of her father's last days, dying from complications of cancer. He was in excruciating pain, suffering, helpless. The hospital would not give him morphine because they said it could cause a heart attack. The man had days, at most weeks, to live. Dear ones felt his pain and their own pain with the sense of helplessness and loss.

When the pain is intense, we can easily lose control, completely identifying with it. If the power of concentration is strong and clinging to the body can be overcome, there is stepping back and resting in peaceful presence. Understandably, this is a tall order—an aspiration.

## EXERCISE

# Making the Best of Pain

Making the best of pain is to accept it so you can respond to it skillfully.

1. Bring your attention to your posture and breath.
2. Open and accept: Step back from the pain to mindfully observe it as if it were not yours.
3. Act:
   - Recognize and acknowledge the pain and its quality.
   - Apply first aid as needed (for example, remove the tack you stepped on, apply antiseptic).
   - Don't identify with the pain. Instead, observe it and the thoughts and feelings triggered by it.
   - Avoid being caught up in a spiral into suffering. You can use a mantra or prayer as a touch stone. (*See the chapter on Working with Sound*)
   - Do what can be done—see a doctor, take a sound bath, take medication, work with the body *(see the chapters on Body and Breath Work),* use a mantra, and be careful and lovingly kind to yourself.
4. Learn: Review the experience and learn from it. Learn what it feels like to step back and observe. Learn to open and accept more easily.

CHAPTER 29

# Managing Anxiety

I am running into more and more people experiencing anxiety as life unfolds amid physical, social, political, and economic uncertainty. Left untreated, anxiety can become chronic, resulting in physical symptoms, behavioral problems, phobias, and addiction. With the right mindset and approach, anxiety can become a wakeup call or just an uninvited visitor you can let in and let go.

> ***Anxiety***: *A felt sense of worry, nervousness, or unease about something with an uncertain outcome. "A mental condition characterized by excessive apprehensiveness about real or perceived threats, typically leading to avoidance behaviors and often to physical symptoms such as increased heart rate and muscle tension."*
> Oxford Dictionary

In some of my earlier work with managing anxiety, I used to focus on intentionally confronting it. But I have since come to embrace two approaches: to *confront* it to treat its roots, and to *avoid* it to treat the immediate experience and reduce physical and behavioral effects. This chapter is about using both approaches.

## Come to Presence

To manage any emotion, you must be self-aware and possess the power to stop, consider, decide, and act. Self-awareness is the ability to step back and observe your feelings and thoughts. It enables presence of mind, responding rather than reacting.

Left unchecked, anxiety can take over, causing panic and becoming chronic. Self-awareness enables you to experience the felt sense of anxiety and be aware of anxious thoughts before they take over and you lose control.

If anxiety does take over, the best you can do is to watch it without adding fuel to the fire by judging yourself or being anxious about being anxious and losing control. Use whatever methods (breathing, aphorisms, etc.), you know and accept help from others to come to presence. Accept and let go to let yourself calm down. Panic episodes pass. The underlying anxiety may still be there, but there is *presence of mind* to remain calm, think clearly, and act sensibly, not being driven by emotions.

Get to know what calm presence feels like so you can step back into it when you start feeling anxious (use the "Take a Breather" exercise in Chapter 5). When you work to increase your self-awareness and emotional intelligence, experiences of anxiety are when that training will kick in.

## Presence of Mind

So, to manage anxiety we need presence of mind.

Presence of mind is a calm state, a step back from the stream of your behavior, thoughts, and feelings. It is being dynamically balanced, in a state of equilibrium in motion, open to whatever comes next. Present—with a sense of serenity, peace, clarity, and comfort—is the platform for skillful action.

## Avoid and Confront

With presence of mind, consider the options: avoid and confront.

*Avoiding* means acknowledging that you need support, so you are not overcome by anxiety. There is nothing wrong with needing

MANAGING ANXIETY

support. It doesn't mean you are weak; it means you are clever and brave enough to seek and accept help when you need it.

*Support* may be in the form of psychotherapy, meditation, mantras*, aphorisms, exercise, analysis, anti-anxiety medication, alcohol, breathwork, or unhealthy habitual behaviors. If it is a choice between being debilitated by anxiety or taking a medication to enable living effectively, I'd take the meds. Be smart about it. Pick supports that cause the least side effects. And don't become habituated or addicted.

The goal is to keep from freaking out so you can reduce or eliminate the anxiety. Once you are centered, you can choose to stay with symptom relief or to confront addressing the root of the anxiety.

Confronting your anxiety means *accepting* physical discomfort and using it to wake up to the beliefs, models, and perceptions that fuel anxiety. Remember: before you can deal with something, you must first acknowledge it. For example, you will want to explore *why* you project doom and gloom, or *why* you tend to worry about scary scenarios and minimize the positive ones.

## Let It Be

The ultimate confrontation is with fear of uncertainty, change, death, and debilitating illness. Confront these and identify with your calm center, confident you will be ready for anything. Then anxiety becomes what Tsoknyi Rinpoche calls a "beautiful monster" that comes and goes. Let it be, but don't serve it tea.

My advice to a person I coach who was freaking out because he was afraid he would never recover from a series of disruptive health issues was:

- You do your best to calm down and listen to what the doctors say.
- You don't need to be a monk or Buddha to be calm in the face of uncertainty and pain.

169

- You know how to sit and follow your breath.
- You know how to allow feelings to be what they are without pushing them away or trying to hide from them.
- You know everything is impermanent and that there will be disappointments, pain, and suffering.
- Anyone in your place would be scared and would want to be well again.
- At this moment, you are doing all you can.
- Clinging to your vision of how things *must* be for you to be happy is bound to make you unhappy.
- Keep your vision of better health and the life you want.
- Do your best to make it happen. But don't cling to it.
- Accept what you can't change.
- Realize that you can handle anything.
- For the moment, take your pain and anxiety meds until you can be calm and present without them.
- Accept and let go.

Cultivate presence with meditation, body and breath work, and other techniques so you can experience it in everything you do, all the time. A calm center is always available; find it and make it the point of origin for your thinking and behavior.

CHAPTER 30

# Enjoy Pleasure

*"Praise and blame, gain and loss, pleasure and
sorrow come and go like the wind.
To be happy, rest like a giant tree in the midst of them all."*
The Buddha

Pleasure is as much a part of life as pain. In this chapter, we explore how to incorporate pleasure into our path to optimal living.

Pleasure is a subjective felt sense that feels good. It promotes enjoyment and happy satisfaction, though attachment to it, wanting to keep it or get more of it, causes suffering. Pleasure may be caused by anything: a spoonful of ice cream, the sight of the sunset or a rainbow, sex, doing something nice for someone, a good grade or promotion, or an encounter with a happy baby. How we perceive it depends on our mindset and setting. One person's pleasure may be another's pain or indifference.

There is a wonderful story by O. Henry, *The Gift of the Magi*, in which, to buy a secret Christmas gift for his lover, a man sells his watch to buy her a set of combs for her long hair. She sells her hair to buy him a chain for his watch. While receiving the gifts was pleasurable, the lovers took greater pleasure in their generosity and gratitude, and in the happiness of realizing how precious their love was to each other. Just as easily, however, they might have become caught up in the displeasure of disappointment of having their gifts go unused. Their mindset made all the difference.

## Pleasure Is Temporary

Pleasure, like everything else, is temporary. The wonderful pleasure of the explosion of the first orgasmic experience of a spoonful of ice cream (or whatever turns you on), is short-lived.

You can savor the experience, resting in its afterglow, the ripple effect of the moment of bliss, letting the feeling of deep satisfaction fill your body and mind. AAAAHH! There is no clinging—you rest in the moment, not trying to hold onto anything, not remembering or thinking about the pleasure, fully enjoying each moment.

But all too often the pleasure experience becomes a doorway to dissatisfaction. Through that doorway, you immediately and greedily go for the next spoonful, until the pleasure ebbs as the pain of feeling bloated, guilty, or both replaces it.

Each thought about the experience reduces the experience of the afterglow. Wanting more leads to trying to repeat the pleasure. But it is never quite the same. Comparing to the past and focused on the future, you miss the present moment. You become addicted.

Make part of your intention to love, or at least fully accept, the moment you're in when you can't be in the moment you love (to paraphrase Stephen Stills' song, "Love the One You're With.") Not clinging to the past or trying to relive it, experiencing deep satisfaction in the present, you can fully enjoy pleasure.

## Tantra, Pleasure, and Delayed Gratification

The pleasure principle is that we instinctively seek pleasure and to avoid pain. As children or immature adults, we seek immediate gratification and pleasure right now to relieve an urge. With maturity and a bit of wisdom, we realize it is far more effective to take account of reality and, when appropriate, delay gratification. We use emotional intelligence to manage the urge, to be responsive rather than reactive.

With mindfulness and a sense of contentment, we recognize that the pleasure of being calmly centered is more readily available and satisfying than the temporary pleasure of intense sensual experiences. Our need for intense sensual pleasures is reduced as we find pleasure in small, everyday things, like the sensation of the warm sun or the coolness of water on a sweltering day.

At the same time, the ability to be undistracted, to let go, while experiencing pleasure makes the experience more intense and gratifying.

Pleasure is often underrated in orthodox Buddhism and Christianity alike, while pain is a common topic viewed as a doorway to enlightenment or salvation. Because it is far more difficult to manage the attachment to pleasure than it is to accept pain, many religions promote renunciation to avoid temptation. Renouncing the pleasures of the flesh is demanding work. Indulging without attachment or becoming lost is even more so.

The Tantric approach takes an opposite approach to renunciation. It is a part of Hinduism and Buddhism that dates back thousands of years, teaching that both pleasure and pain are vehicles for enlightenment. In 18th century utilitarianism, a revival of hedonism, it was said that individuals ought to pursue the greatest pleasure. Immersed in pleasure, awake and aware, there is the experience of oneness. Confronting the urges to gain pleasure and avoid pain is spiritual work.

Tantra is a tradition often associated with sexual practices, though it is something beyond that; it is a weaving together of the physical with the spiritual. A tantric approach attempts to attain freedom while living in the world and experiencing the fulness of life. Instead of taking a renunciative approach, which views pleasure as a trap to be avoided, the Tantric way embraces everything.

Tantra is about using all experience as a means for bringing powerful subtle energy up from the lower energies of physical pleasure to transform it into bliss beyond sensuality. Since sexual experience is so powerful in and of itself, it has been used as a vehicle for this transformation. The practitioner learns to exercise physical and mental control to make that transformation.

But sex is not the only vehicle for this kind of experience. Eating a perfect peach or having a cold beer on a hot day also offer moments of pleasure.

## EXERCISE
### Tantric Practice/Tantric Non-Dual Practice

- Find or imagine a partner who harmonizes with you.
- Engage or visualize you and your partner in an intimate embrace
- Melt into one another so that any distinction between the two is erased. You are one in the experience of pleasure that comes from merging with the other.
- Dissolve into awareness free of the ego-identity and distractions that obstruct the experience of union. Let go into and with the other.

No self. Awareness. Union. Bliss.

Sharing this meditation with another is powerful, but if that is not practical you can conjure up an imaginary partner with whom you share that sense of deep resonant harmony.

The meditative experience is a taste of union in awareness. Weave together the physical and spiritual. Be open to tastes in daily life. Each time you realize you have fallen asleep in distractions, awakening is a taste of union. Do this repeatedly, until the moment of tantric unity expands to become the way you experience the world.

CHAPTER 31

# Revealing the Mind: Psychedelics and Psychotherapy

*"Until you make the unconscious conscious, it will direct your life and you will call it fate. One does not become enlightened by (only) imagining figures of light but by making the dark conscious."*
Carl Jung

This chapter discusses mind-revealing experiences, experiences that bring the subconscious to consciousness and go beyond ordinary conceptual thinking to test our mental models and worldview.

The word "psychedelic" is derived from the Greek word *delos*, which means "clear" or "manifest," and the root *psych*, which means "mind." So "psychedelic" is interpreted as "mind-revealing."

With that interpretation, the entire path toward optimal living can be understood as a psychedelic, mind-revealing experience. The path is a process of accepting what we find when the subconscious is brought to consciousness. The peaceful warrior makes use of insights gained in mind-revealing experiences to enhance functional and spiritual intelligence.

It takes courage and care to reveal the subconscious and take on new ways of thinking. It might be scary at first but then it becomes a great relief to discover that the solid self you have been working so hard to hold onto is really a process. You realize it is all a movie unfolding and accept that, while you exert some influence on the script, you are not in control.

Mind-revealing experiences are a means for cultivating and exercising our old friends: self-awareness, acceptance, and letting go. Applying these gives access to the mind's inner workings.

However, it is important to be on a firm psychological foundation before going into "mystical" realms that break with conventional definitions of reality. You need a healthy ego to go beyond ego. Be careful when you are working to change your mind. At the same time, push the edge of your capacity to let go.

## Psychedelic Experience

There is a resurgence in interest in psychedelic experiences using substances like LSD and psilocybin. Some want the experience for the fun of it. Some want quick fixes to break through and see the light. Others find these experiences therapeutic in opening the mind to better manage stress, trauma, and emotional issues. Over thousands of years, psychedelic experiences have been skillfully used in spiritual rituals to gain self-knowledge under supportive conditions by intentionally letting go.

More recently, with a foundation of scientific studies that goes back to research in the 1950s and '60s, evidence is emerging that psychedelic experiences can be useful not only in the treatment of addiction, depression, and post-traumatic stress, but also in the pursuit of wellness.

> *"Studies suggest that psychedelics may facilitate neuroplasticity at the cellular and network levels, allowing the brain to form and reorganize connection. While every experience does that, psychedelic experiences do it to change the perception of self.*

## REVEALING THE MIND: PSYCHEDELICS AND PSYCHOTHERAPY

> *This creates a unique opportunity to change patterns in brain activity, and in turn, improve symptoms, behavior, and functioning, to ultimately eliminate suffering."*[47]

(Check the footnote[48] for references that will give you a deeper sense of the subject and some of the underlying neurological structures that result in changes to perception.)

Mind-revealing experiences can be brought on by taking psychedelic substances, doing intense meditations, yoga, and engaging in psychotherapy or extreme activities. They may occur spontaneously as you gradually accept and let go.

Whether you use drugs, meditations, or other means, do it skillfully as a learning experience. We want to go beyond the conceptual mind, *not* lose it. You are in uncharted territory when you first confront your perceptions and beliefs, look deeply into who you are, and confront challenging emotions.

---

[47] Center for the Neuroscience of Psychedelics, Massachusetts General Hospital https://www.massgeneral.org/psychiatry/treatments-and-services/center-for-the-neuroscience-of-psychedelics#:~:text=Studies%20suggest%20that%20psychedelics%20may,functioning%2C%20to%20ultimately%20eliminate%20suffering.

[48] The following are sample references to more in-depth discussions of psychedelics, for more, search the web. There are many studies, articles, and videos from researchers and others that address the neurological effects of psychedelics and their effects on mental health

1. Pollan, Michael, *How to Change Your Mind: The New Science of Psychedelics*, London: Penguin Books, 2019.
2. *How to Change Your Mind* docuseries https://www.netflix.com/title/80229847
3. Ly, Calvin, et al, "Psychedelics Promote Structural and Functional Neural Plasticity" August 8, 2018, https://www.ncbi.nlm.nih.gov/pmc/articles/PMC6082376/#S3title
4. Leary, Timothy, *Psychedelic Experience: A Manual Based on the Tibetan Book of the Dead*, S.l.: Citadel PR, 2021.

Confronting the subconscious can be scary. While some fully enjoy the freedom gained by breaking out of the confines of their conditioned mind, others panic when the stories, beliefs, and models that are the foundation for their life as they know it dissolve. Some suffer long-term negative effects. So be careful. Work with a guide and in a supportive setting. Avoid using drugs, therapies, and other practices as habit-forming escapes from "reality." *(See the chapter on "Working with Emotions.")*

As with anything you encounter, ground or center yourself with breath and body awareness, let go of expectations, and accept whatever is happening, knowing it is all a temporary projection of your own mind, and that you will be fine.

Again, there is no need to ingest psychedelic substances like LSD or psilocybin to reveal the mind. The peaceful warrior reveals the mind when he or she engages in devotional practice, psychotherapy, ingests concepts, and uses methods to look at the mind's inner workings. With psychedelic substances, once you have taken it you are committed for a few hours. When working with psychotherapy or meditation, it is easy to stop, but even with these, once the mind opens to reveal its nature, there is no turning back.

## Set and Setting

Your perception of any experience depends on your mindset (set) and setting. "Set denotes the preparation of the individual, including his personality structure and his mood at the time. Setting is physical—the weather, the room's atmosphere, social—feelings of persons present toward one another, and cultural—prevailing views as to what is real."[49]

---

[49] Leary, Timothy, Metzner, Alpert, *The Psychedelic Experience*, ePenguin Classiocs,, 2008, p.3.

## REVEALING THE MIND: PSYCHEDELICS AND PSYCHOTHERAPY

> *"You must be able to accept the possibility that there is a limitless range of awareness for which we now have no words, that awareness can expand beyond the range of your ego, yourself, your familiar identity, beyond everything you have learned, beyond your notions of space and time, beyond the differences which usually separate people from each other and from the world around them."*[50]

With acceptance of these basic trusts and beliefs, you can experience a breakthrough to a new perspective on the nature of your mind and relationship to your environment.

As for setting, you can be anywhere you feel safe, secure, confident, and comfortable. Make sure you are with people you trust and that you can rely on someone—a guide, therapist, or coach—to help you should you need it.

With the right set and setting, your mind-revealing experience can give you a sense of what it is like to be free of unfounded beliefs and models, with a revised understanding of self. Take this into daily life and cultivate the ability to make every experience mind revealing.

---

[50] Ibid, p. 5.

## EXERCISE
## Revealing the Mind

Make note of your answers to the following questions and review over time.

How does it feel when a belief you have relied on is found to be "wrong"—not in synch with your experience?

When you are faced with a situation you don't understand and can't control how do you react? Do you let go and enjoy the experience or try to hold on to "rationality"?

How often do you let go into whatever is happening and rest in awareness?

How often do you hold yourself back?

CHAPTER 32

# Devotion

*"Your daily life is your temple and your religion.
When you enter into it take with you your all."*
Kahlil Gibran

This chapter presents devotion as part of the path. Authentic devotional experience is a non-conceptual experience of surrendering—accepting and letting go. It is mind revealing.

Devotion is one of five basic yogic approaches. The devotee becomes one with a devotional object—God, the universal force, truth, spiritual teaching, higher self, nature, humanity, a saint, or guru.

Conventional devotion is love, loyalty, or enthusiasm for someone or something. Depending on the object, it can motivate skillful behavior and dedication to values like wisdom, loyalty, compassion, and kindness. Conventional devotion can create a sense of safety, of being taken care of. It can also lead to blind belief, reinforce a sense of separation and hierarchy, and strengthen the sense of a solid ego.

In the mystical sense, devotion is an expression of unconditional love and surrender. Devotion is a doorway into realization of wisdom and compassion.

*"The whole point about devotion—not blind faith or blind devotion but complete devotion . . . is that ego cannot take part in it."*
Chogyam Trungpa Rinpoche

## Devotional Practice

Devotional practice is performed to open the heart and experience one's calm center and the spaciousness it opens to.

In the Jewish mystical tradition, there is *kavanah*, Hebrew for "intention" or "sincere feeling." It is the mindset that aligns mind, heart, and intention in prayer and rituals. It is heartfelt emotional devotion and absorption. There is also *shekinah*, the glory of divine presence. In the Hindu traditions, there is *bhav*, a felt sense of passionate immersion in the moment. In Christianity, there is the experience of the Holy Spirit. In Islam, there are mystic dances or chants to not only worship, but to experience oneness. Regardless of the religion, devotional practice separates concepts and interpretations from felt experience so the devotee can live life in touch with the divine.

There are many devotional practices. One is the day-to-day practice of selflessly serving others.

> *"There is always the danger that we may just do the work for the sake of the work. This is where the respect and the love and the devotion come in—that we do it to God, to Christ, and that's why we try to do it as beautifully as possible."*
> Mother Teresa

> *"As you love your own body, so regard everyone as equal to your own body. When the Supreme Experience supervenes, everyone's service is revealed as one's own service. Call it a bird, an insect, an animal, or a man, call it by any name you please, one serves one's own Self in every one of them. "*
> Anandamayi Ma

In devotion, the servant and the served are God. Being devoted to God and seeing everyone as God, there is a natural expression of compassionate action and a commitment to perfect service. The ego is dissolved in God. The devotee experiences non-dual awareness, union. God is serving God.

There are also many formal devotional practices—meditations, prayer, chanting, singing, dance, and rituals. In the Vajryana Buddhist tradition, the practice of Guru Yoga leads to the same end as selfless service—experiencing awareness or love beyond concept. The practice elicits the experience of the inseparability of the relative relationship between oneself and the devotional object (the guru) and the absolute merging and dissolving of the self.

In this practice, the practitioner chooses an object, usually a deity, saint, guru, or symbol. The practice is to merge with and take on the object's attributes, like, wisdom, compassion, healing, courage, fierceness, etc.

For example, the enlightened female Buddha Tara is the embodiment of wisdom and compassion; she is both peaceful and wrathful with the attribute of great, persistent courage. She is revered as the nurturer and protector of spiritual travelers.

Visualizing the deity and its attributes, one brings its energy to the moment; one prays to and opens to the deity's power. Some will be satisfied with that. But taking it to the next level, the practitioner merges with the deity, doing away with any sense of separation from the divine. Then, taking it to the ultimate level, the practitioner dissolves into empty, non-dual, open, boundless clarity.

Ritual can be a powerful tool that takes the practitioner beyond the intellect to experience and from experience to spiritual awakening. Just as easily, it can become rote and empty of meaning.

The difference is the way one lets go into the ritual or spiritual practice. Learn it. Stop thinking about it. Just do it. Then experience what it has to teach. Let go into the mystical experience.

If you are interested in cultivating devotion, I recommend researching and connecting with a spiritual or mystical teaching tradition that recognizes the power of devotion and includes it in its approach. *(See the chapter on "Community.")*

Question everything. Beware of bypassing emotions and hiding from the reality of change and uncertainty. Beware of charlatans and ego-centric gurus.

## Aversion

Questioning is useful, but unskillful doubt can lead to aversion to religion and mystical experience. Aversion is a wake-up call. Investigate its cause and whether you want to overcome it. In this case, experience the power of devotion by using it skillfully, avoiding the pitfalls of blind belief and emotional bypass.

For me, aversion to religion came from early experiences with teachers who left out the mystical and instead cultivated a sense of closed-minded belief and divisiveness. Through study in Marxist and other atheistic philosophies, I came to see religion as an opiate used to dull the pain of life and soothe the masses. But, as I experienced the results of yoga, meditation, chanting, ritual practices, and teachings that reconciled logical thinking and mystical experience, I came to see devotional practice as a vehicle for promoting wisdom, love, and compassion, and replacing egocentric behavior with ethical behavior.

Let's not throw the baby out with the bathwater. As a peaceful warrior, like the swan that separates milk from water, extract the essence from the religion and leave the rest behind.

## EXERCISE

## Devotion

Imagine being a god who chooses to give up existence as a god—its "godness"—and take a form on earth, subject to the pains of existence as a mortal.

This is the peak of selfless service, a theme found in many religious traditions. It is one of the more radical expressions of devotion: all-powerful Lord Shiva coming to Earth as Hanuman, the servant of Ram, the incarnation of Vishnu, the protector. Jehovah incarnating as Jesus, the servant-savior of man. A *bodhisattva* in Buddhism, an awakened one who gives up their own enlightenment to take human birth to help all sentient beings awaken.

How does the subject of devotion, selfless service, and mystical experience inform your efforts to live well and perform optimally?

Are you averse to or attracted to religion, spirituality, and mysticism? Why?

CHAPTER 33

# Working with Emotions

*"If your emotional abilities aren't in hand, if you don't have self-awareness, if you are not able to manage your distressing emotions, if you can't have empathy and have effective relationships, then no matter how smart you are, you are not going to get very far."*
Daniel Goleman

*"I've learned that people will forget what you said, people will forget what you did, but people will never forget how you made them feel."*
Maya Angelou

Previous chapters have provided techniques for sharpening mindfulness, concentration, and body awareness as well as opening the mind and heart. This chapter applies these to working with emotions.

Emotions and the way they affect our lives are complex. Working with or managing them requires understanding and putting emotions in their right place, fully integrated into daily life. It requires:

- Recognizing emotions
- Accepting and experiencing them fully
- Stepping back so you don't identify with them
- Having rational expectations
- Applying patient effort with courage and compassion

An emotion is a feeling, a felt sense. It is a state of mind different from reason or knowledge, a reaction to circumstances, conditioning, mood, and relationships. Emotional reactions release chemicals in the brain, which are experienced as strong physical feelings, usually toward a specific person, event, or object.

Emotions are triggered by an event—for example, someone does or says something threatening or you are faced with a tight deadline you might not meet. The trigger ignites some internal condition and the internal condition (for example, some past experiences or beliefs) causes fear or anger to come up. *(As stated in the chapter "Mindful of Processes," "the process is so fast that it seems immediate.")*

Emotions of all kinds will occur. Anxiety, fear, depression, jealousy, and anger are the primary "afflictive" or painful emotions we face. "Positive" emotions include joy, interest, contentment, pride, and love. They feel good.

When any of the emotions take over the mind and drive reactive behavior, the results are pain and suffering in the form of poor decisions, broken relationships, unnecessary conflict, and physical distress. Emotions take over and drive behavior when we try to rid ourselves of the painful and keep the pleasant feelings. *(The chapters on "Making the Best of Pain" and "Enjoy Pleasure" look into the way pain and pleasure affect us and can be worked with the same basic approach is applied to emotions.)*

Suppressed emotions emerge as chronic suffering. While we do not want to be driven by emotions, we do not want to suppress them. Suppressed or bypassed emotions lead to just as much—if not more—pain, only over a longer time. Even the most effective meditative and psychological methods can be used for spiritual bypass to avoid delving into the more difficult emotions.

Working with emotions means to avoid being driven by them while fully feeling, acknowledging, understanding, and giving them their place as natural experiences. It also means disconnecting the triggers from the firing mechanism that ignites the emotion.

## Managing Emotions—Applying Emotional Intelligence

Working with emotions applies emotional intelligence—self-awareness and self-management—to be able to recognize emotions and to choose what to do with them.

In my experience, I have worked to respond to rather than react to frustration and anger, for example pounding my desk or raising my voice when frustrated. Patient effort made it possible to overcome that habitual reaction. Not to say that I don't ever become angry, I do. But when I feel the anger rising, I can step back and find a moment of calm. I might slip into habit, but not for long. And when I do, I can learn from the experience and renew my resolve to accept and let go.

The general instruction, no matter what the emotion, is to accept the feelings, find a moment of calm, and let go before lashing out in anger, withdrawing in fear, or obsessing jealously. Here the letting go is not letting the emotion take over but letting go of the attachment that has caused the emotion. Open to fear or anger and allow it to be there, even though it feels terrible. The reaction is an attempt to avoid the feelings

If you can't stop the reaction, accept that. And after it's over, analyze to find underlying causes so you can cut the connection between the trigger and the reaction.

## Applying Remedies

Once you can step back and mindfully observe an emotion as a complex of physical sensations, it loses its power and passes. If it doesn't move on as quickly as you'd like, you can apply coping remedies to relieve the symptoms—for example, disengaging and running around the block to blow off steam, diverting your attention, or using the breath or other centering and relaxation techniques like music or a mantra to calm yourself down. It can be something as simple as touching your thumb to your forefinger to bring you into your body and your calm center.

If the situation is extreme and recurring, and relaxation and centering techniques are not working, you might do well to engage in psychotherapy and, under supervision, use medications to change the brain chemistry that is causing the emotional sensations. Cognitive and meditative techniques can then be applied to remove the need for the medication over time.

But beware. Avoid letting coping techniques, including meditation and psychotherapy, become habits used to bypass emotions. Avoid feeling guilty or like a failure for having to resort to coping when you think you should be free of emotional reactions.

It takes practice. If at first you don't succeed, keep trying. Be patient, forgiving, and kind to yourself. Keep in mind that your goal is to both accept the emotion, and to accept when you are not yet ready to accept and let go.

Think of your emotions and your reactions to them as visitors. They are Tsoknyi Rinpoche's "beautiful monsters." Be okay with the feeling. Welcome it as a visitor. But don't encourage it to stay. Don't feed it with obsessive thoughts and stories that fuel your worries.

*Everything, including the deepest emotions and our reactions to them are momentary experiences, illusory but not to be denied.*

### EXERCISE
# Managing Emotions

Think about how you manage your emotions. Write down and reflect on the following:

What coping techniques do you use to manage your emotions? How frequently do you use them? Have they become habits you use to avoid or bypass your emotions?

When you analyze the causes of your emotions, do you find that attachment and aversion are root causes?

When you become lost in emotional reactivity, do you easily forgive yourself and commit to getting it right in the future?

Try the RAIN technique when an emotion arises:

- Recognize it
- Accept it
- Investigate where it is in the body and what it feels like
- Non-identification. Don't identify with it and don't judge it; observe it and let it pass.

CHAPTER 34

# Working in Relationships

*"All life is relationship. To be is to be related."*
J. Krishnamurthy

*"Everything that irritates us about others can lead
us to an understanding of ourselves."*
Carl Gustav Jung

There are many relationships in our life—casual, business, romantic, familial, social, ones with those we like and dislike, and the one with our self—and all of them influence happiness and effectiveness. As you probably know, relationships are complex, always changing, and challenging.

It should be no surprise that *being centered, self-aware, calm, and accepting* is the way to healthy relationships in which emotional reactivity is replaced by responsiveness.

This chapter applies meditation techniques, body awareness, and the ability to work with pleasure and pain to relationships. It explores *relationship yoga* as a means for engaging in and sustaining healthy relationships. It makes relationships fertile ground for cultivating wellness.

## The Psychology of Relationships

There are thousands of books on the psychology of relationships. Here the focus is on:

- how relationships affect the way we feel and behave
- how the way we feel and behave affects our relationships
- how we can use our relationships as fertile ground for self-awareness, acceptance, and letting go.

Relationships affect and are affected by our feelings and behaviors. Psychologically, some relationships create the conditioning and neuroses which come out in other relationships as we unconsciously play out past relationship patterns.

Our attachments make opening to healthy relationships difficult. We want to protect ourselves from being taken advantage of. We want the spark of romantic love to last forever, our lover/partner/friend to change, to stay the same, to be more perfect. Jealousy and fear arise. We might confuse a boss, employee, or significant other with a parent, sibling, or child. We might seek protection and certainty and believe they can be attained in a relationship.

Working on yourself in your relationships is practicing relationship yoga—using self-awareness, acceptance, and letting go in relationships to dissolve the obstacles in the way of experiencing wellness. Relationship yoga brings awareness to the relationship so you can acknowledge inner workings while not being driven by them. The concept is to work on yourself in your relationships so you can open to your inner self and others.

## What a Healthy Relationship Is

Before getting into how to practice relationship yoga, let's define what we are after: healthy relationships. A healthy relationship satisfies. There is respect, honesty, effective communication, a sense of safety, give and take, and a recognition of both independence and interdependence. Emotions, faults, failures, conflicts, and all the rest of the relationship challenges are accepted and worked through.

An unhealthy relationship is missing one or more of the qualities of a healthy relationship. It is characterized by a lack of honest, open communication. One or more of the partners lack self-awareness. There are unrealistic expectations and an unwillingness or inability to work on the things that get in the way. Empathy and compassion are missing.

You can even maintain a healthy relationship with someone you dislike, who may be abusive or just boring. You don't have to hang out with them. You can love and respect them from afar. But if you must be with them, protect yourself and use the experience to explore how you can grow from the relationship. Don't add fuel to the fire. Become centered. Cultivate patience, empathy, lovingkindness, and compassion. Protect yourself from abuse. As scary as it may seem, you can choose how much unhealthiness you are willing to take and what you will do about it.

## Working with Relationships: Relationship Yoga

Relationship yoga uses relationships as a vehicle for cultivating wellness.

Working with relationships seeks to transform the drama of interpersonal relationship into opportunity for dropping away the obstacles to both opening to others and satisfying personal needs for safety and satisfaction.

To work on and with relationships, acknowledge that most of us are imperfect. Then make your relationships gyms, classrooms, *ashrams*\*, and yoga studios for working on yourself, confronting, and dropping away all the things that get in the way of connecting, or disconnecting, with others lovingly and compassionately.

A guy I know is intelligent, knowledgeable, self-centered, and belligerent. He verbally abuses people publicly, yelling, demeaning, threatening, and insulting. He seems unable to control his anger. His self-centered belligerence makes being in relationship with him unpleasant.

Another person is so without sensitivity to others that he goes on and on about himself and his ideas with no concern for the other people around him. Others are dishonest, unable to share their feelings, unaware of how their mood or behavior affects others. Some are so eager to avoid conflict and please that they agree to things that are not in their best interest. Others are judgmental and blaming while some are incapable of taking criticism.

When encountering these characteristics (in yourself and others), mindfully experience your thoughts and feelings. Realize that the other guy's anger or insensitivity is his problem. Your responsibility is the way you behave. Let the vibrations, waves of feelings, flow through you. In healthy relationships, partners help one another, confronting issues as one rather than confronting one another. *(See the chapter on "Working with Emotions.")*

Note that practicing relationship yoga is not a cure all for managing conflict and negotiations. The fact is that a hostile adversary without boundaries can make progress impossible. When you work to be free from your own reactivity you are better able to manage the situation

> *"If we can realize that it is not how another acts that is of primary importance, but how each one of us acts and reacts, and that if that reaction and action can be fundamentally, deeply understood— then relationship will undergo a deep and radical change."*[51]
> J. Krishnamurti

---

[51] "Relationship Is a Process of Self-Revelation," Krishnamurti Foundation of America, https://bos.etapestry.com/prod/viewEmailAsPage.do?erRef =517.0.786061382&databaseId=KrishnamurtiFoundationofAme&maili

## Opening to Others

Relationship yoga brings with it the awareness of oneness and interdependence. It uses the sense of the Hindu greeting, *Namaste*. It is a great centering technique (like taking a Breather) that you can use in everyday life.

The traditional Hindu greeting is saying, "*Namaste*," with hands together at the chest and a slight bow. Of course, you don't have to say the word or bow in a certain way. A nod, a smile, a handshake, whatever is culturally appropriate, will do. It is the intention you bring that is important.

On the surface, saying, "*Namaste,*" is simply a greeting of respect. A deeper meaning is, *I greet that which is in you that is also in me.* It is an acknowledgment that in our hearts we are one, we are interdependent, and we all may be driven by mental habits, biases, and neuroses.

The hands pressed together at the center of the chest is a yoga posture or *mudra* that means "offering." This simple gesture elicits a sense of composure, of returning to the heart where everything is always just fine. It is a posture that connects your right and left brain, unifying your active and receptive qualities in balance. You are offering your essence, your love to the other, recognizing their divinity and how it is the same as yours.

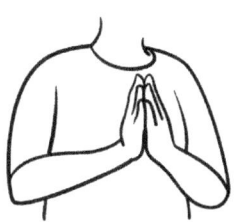

---

ngId=42218567&jobRef=517.0.923185219&key=2f2025ae2e57e7184329 8d80bed5cfde&personaRef=517.0.786061384&memberId=1579854876. Accessed April 21, 2023.

### EXERCISE

## Greeting

Greet people you encounter with *Namaste* in mind. Briefly, just for a second, silently in your own mind, no mudra necessary, remind yourself of the wisdom of opening and acceptance. You can add a visualization of the *mudra* and bow to intensify the exercise. It is a lovely way to begin any encounter. It is the foundation for healthy relationships, even ones with people you don't like.

Note in your journal how it feels as you first start practicing the technique and whether it becomes more natural over time.

Are there barriers to using the technique?

Does it work to center yourself?

Does being centered and open help in the relationship?

CHAPTER 35

# Applying Relationship Yoga

*The best thing you can do for yourself and others is to work on yourself. And there's no better place to work on yourself than in your relationships.*

This chapter focuses on applications of relationship yoga in managing life situations.

## Empathy, Lovingkindness, and Compassion

In the chapter on "Wisdom," we noted that wise intention expresses itself as persistence, courage, resilience, empathy, kindness, and compassion. These contribute to healthy relationships and the ability to make the best of challenging situations.

Here we'll focus on empathy (understanding or feeling what others are experiencing), kindness (wishing yourself and others to be well), and compassion (the desire and action to alleviate suffering). These qualities contribute to healthy relationships, and relationships are where we can cultivate them.

Empathy, kindness, and compassion enable addressing relationship challenges with understanding, forgiveness, effectively managing conflict, and setting reasonable and rational expectations.

Empathy and compassion are closely related. Three types of empathy have been identified by well-respected psychologists Daniel Goleman and Paul Ekman: *cognitive* (understanding what another person is feeling by taking their perspective), *emotional* (feeling with the other, experiencing their emotion as if it were contagious), and *compassionate* (upon understanding and feeling, there is a spontaneous urge to help). This last type of empathy has been referred to as compassion, literally "to suffer together" with the motivation to relieve the suffering.

Mindful of inner processes, we can balance the three kinds of empathy to act without being driven by our emotions. We can protect ourselves and be open-minded and open-hearted.

Where empathy is about understanding, feeling, and doing, lovingkindness is wishing that oneself and others are well—happy, healthy, prosperous, and free of unnecessary suffering. Acting with kindness—friendly, generous, considerate—is natural when you are centered and remember that we are all one.

## Managing Conflict[52]

Conflicts are opportunities to apply empathy, kindness, and compassion to work on oneself and to strengthen relationships. If there are no conflicts, it is a sign that the relationship might be in trouble. When conflicts are not resolved in a healthy way, relationships suffer.

In relationship yoga, the approach is to confront the conflict rather than one another, to seek win-win resolutions whenever possible. Even if the other party is unwilling to collaborate, explore the conflict rationally:

- Exercise empathy and seek to understand where the other is coming from.

---

[52] For a full treatment of managing conflict see Pitagorsky, George, *Managing Conflict in Projects: Applying Mindfulness and Analysis for Optimal Results*, Project Management Institute, Inc., 2012. The approach works well in or outside of projects.

- Identify your needs, your wants, and the possibility that you can derive what you need even if it doesn't come in the way you want it.
- Practice lovingkindness; intend to take care of yourself as well as the other.
- Don't let your emotions drive your behavior.
- Remember, in most cases, your relationship will go on after the conflict, so avoid insults, threats, power plays, and other tactics that are likely to make things worse in the long run.

Observe your beliefs and biases and how they affect the conflict and relationship. Are you holding on to anything that you can accept and let go of? Are your emotions getting in the way of reason and mutual benefit?

## Managing Expectations[53]

Conflict is a challenge in all relationships. With empathy and lovingkindness as a base, it becomes possible to manage conflict effectively, so each conflict contributes to strengthening the relationship.

Unstated, unrealistic, or misunderstood expectations are often at the root of conflict. We expect one thing; they expect another. When either is disappointed, there is conflict.

Here is a story to highlight the importance of expectations in relationships:

> *"My friend, Mary, told me about planning a kayak trip with a friend along the coast of Maine. The friend was quite fit and had a sleek kayak while Mary was less fit and had a borrowed, slower boat.*

---

[53] For a full treatment of managing expectations, see Pitagorsky, George, *Managing Expectations: A Mindful Approach to Achieving Success*, Key Step Media, 2017.

*"Once the trip started, there was discord. Mary's friend expected an average day's travel to be about fifteen miles, while a good day for Mary was around seven miles. Mary was always way behind. This left Mary feeling discouraged while her friend was frustrated and impatient.*

*"Had they discussed their expectations in advance of the trip, they would have come to an agreement about how many miles they'd paddle each day and at what pace. Or they would have agreed to disagree and found other kayaking partners or done something else."*[54]

To achieve mutually understood expectations, we should communicate, push back, and give in when appropriate. Apply the basics—observe thoughts and feelings, accept, and let go. The goal is to make sure expectations are not only explicit and mutually understood but rational as well. Rational expectations recognize that:

- The impossible is impossible.
- Everything is subject to change.
- Everything is interconnected—changes cause a ripple effect.
- Estimates are estimates, not actual outcomes.
- Expectations must be explicit and mutually understood.

How does it feel when your expectations are met, and not met? How does it affect your relationships? What do you need to do to make expectations mutually understood and rational?

Keep in mind that when you bring expectations to the surface, you may find they are irreconcilably different, which may make the relationship unworkable in its current or desired form. Better to know that as early as possible to avoid ongoing conflict and disappointment.

---

[54] Pitagorsky, George, *Managing Expectations: A Mindful Approach to Achieving Success*, Key Step Media, 2017.

## Forgiveness

Forgiveness is another element in managing conflict. The overriding method to achieve sustainable wellness is acceptance and letting go. Forgiveness is a form of accepting and letting go. In relationships we may cause harm or feel we have been harmed by the words or actions of others. We may hold onto self-judgment.

> *"'Forgiveness does not mean condoning a harmful action, or denying injustice or suffering,' writes meditation teacher Sharon Salzberg. 'It should never be confused with being passive toward violation or abuse. Forgiveness is an inner relinquishment of guilt or resentment, both of which are devastating to us in the end.'"*[55]

The message is to let go of guilt and resentment because they are harmful and do no good. If tension and difficult emotions are confronted, work with them to keep yourself from being driven by them.

Practice relationship yoga, using each relationship and each conflict as opportunities for self-awareness and growth.

---

[55] "5 Timeless Teachings on Extending Forgiveness to Ourselves and Others: Buddhist Wisdom on Cultivating a Merciful Heart," *Tricycle*, March 15, 2022, https://tricycle.org/trikedaily/forgiveness-teachings/?utm_source =Tricycle&utm_campaign=e81577caed-Newsletter_22_3_26_NS&utm_ medium=email&utm_term=0_1641abe55e-e81577caed-307270717

### EXERCISE
# Lovingkindness Meditation

This exercise is a mindfulness and concentration meditation technique to cultivate lovingkindness and come in touch with resistance to opening the heart. At first, the process may feel contrived. But after a while of "faking it" and observing the thoughts and feelings that arise and stand in your way, you let go of the thinking and allow your heart to open so you feel loving and kind.

Each practice session can be anywhere from five to 30 minutes or more. In a quiet, comfortable spot, take a comfortably erect posture, and bring attention to the body and breath to calm the mind. When you are ready, one by one, bring to mind people you love, yourself, and others, including ones you dislike. For each, slowly repeat and imagine waves of lovingkindness bathing them. Replace the word "they" with the person's name and image:

> May (I, they) be happy.
> May (I, they) live in peace and ease.
> May (I, they) receive all they need.
> May (I, they) be healthy and free of suffering.
> May (I, they) be free of the causes of suffering.
> May all beings be free of suffering and of the causes of suffering.

After each session, ask yourself: *Is that easy?* Is there any resistance to being loving and kind to yourself?

How does it feel when you wish good things to people you don't like? Can you be empathetic and open your heart to them, even if you never like what they do or did?

You can mix lovingkindness meditation with other meditation techniques or use it exclusively for a period. To experience the full effect of lovingkindness meditation, work up to 20 minutes or more per session. As with other methods, also apply it informally, for a few seconds, when you meet or think about someone. *Namaste.*

CHAPTER 36

# Working at Work—Right Livelihood

*"When we get too caught up in the busyness of the world, we lose connection with one another—and ourselves."*
Jack Kornfield

Working on mind and body—using meditative techniques and concepts like self-awareness, acceptance, and letting go—is applied in relationships. Relationship yoga is applied not only in intimate and familial relationships, but also in the way you earn a living and the way you live in community with others.

In this chapter, the focus is on applying the work on your mind, body, emotions, and relationships to the way you work.

## Work

Work is effort expended to achieve an outcome. It is the tasks and projects you perform, whether you are paid for them or not. While it includes the work you do on yourself, here we focus on the work you do while you are working on yourself.

You may work at a job, manage a portfolio, volunteer, do household chores, make whoever is supporting you happy, or deal with the fear of becoming homeless. You may enjoy the privilege of being able to go on extended vacations or regularly spend a couple of hundred dollars on a dinner.

You might love the work you do, or not. Ideally, your livelihood and your passion coincide. You make a living, and you are satisfied by your work. If you are not blessed with that, it is an opportunity for you to make the best of your situation by using it to cut through attachment, aversion, and ignorance.

Work is like any other part of life's journey: a place to practice accepting and letting go.

Remember accepting and letting go. If you don't like the way things are, change them if you can; accept them if you can't. You can always change your mindset and attitude, and manage your emotions and relationships. You may be able to find a new job or just quit your current one and go traveling. You can talk to your boss and coworkers.

Before you do anything, figure out what is contributing to the unhappiness. Are you bringing attachment, unfounded beliefs, and biases to your job? Remember, wherever you go, there you are. If you change jobs or partners and find that the conditions repeat, look within. What expectations, attitudes, or neuroses have you brought with you?

## A Story

I recently went to pick up a CD (yes, they still exist) of my wife's MRI results. The people in the office looked in four separate places for the disk. Finally, the guy at the computer found that the disk had not yet been created. He then made the CD.

While waiting, I commented that putting them always in the same place would save them lots of time. He said, "Easier said than done. We have a coworker who refuses to follow procedures and can't be relied upon. She's really hard to work with."

She wasn't present, so I couldn't hear her side of the story. Imagine having to spend several hours a day working with someone like that!

In a situation like this, can you practice relationship yoga and do what is possible to change the situation? If there is no way to relieve the pain, can you ask for a transfer or quit?

But what if there is no possibility of escape? Then what? The simple answer is, "Make the best of it."

As with any challenge, find your center and work from there, emanating subtle waves of lovingkindness, compassion, and joy. Do your best to avoid being dragged into angry resentment or non-caring.

## Work-Life Balance

*"A weekend? What is a weekend?"*
Spoken by the Dowager Countess in *Downton Abbey*

Even when the people you are working with are nice and competent, maintaining a healthy balance between work and the rest of life contributes to wellness. If you can, craft—in the context of your job, culture, family status, and sensibilities—a balance that works for you and those around you.

There are many choices. A 5:2 work-to-life ratio is five weekdays and two weekend days. Why not a 3:4 ratio or 4:3? Look at the balance across a month or year rather than a week. Can your situation permit working seven consecutive days and taking off the next four, followed by another stint of work, etc.? Can you work intensively for a month or two and then take a few weeks off? Consider how vacation/holidays and long weekends factor into the balance.

Consider the balance during the workday. How much time do you devote to work: is it four, seven, 14 hours? Can you intersperse personal chores and take time for relaxation, meditation, socializing, childcare, volunteer work, and physical exercise?

How much time do you allocate for work on non-workdays? Will you check your business email? Will you think about work issues and make a note when the solution to your most challenging problem pops up while showering or playing ping-pong?

With an open and realistic mind, craft a balance that makes you healthy, wealthy, and wise.

There may or may not be room for negotiation and you may choose to live with things as they are—trading off security, social acceptance, and responsibilities to family and community for personal likes and dislikes. Accept and let go.

EXERCISE

## Mindfulness at Work

Work on yourself at work. Integrate working with your mind, body, emotions, and relationships.

Practice mindfulness meditation with informal meditation practices, like Breathers and body posture awareness.

Take the 40-day challenge. Choose a technique: Breathers, *namaste* thinking, lovingkindness meditation, posture awareness, or breath awareness. Use an alarm to remind you to take a mini meditation break every half-hour.

CHAPTER 37

# Community—Friends on the Path

*"Our seemingly separate lives become meaningful as we discover how truly necessary we are to each other."*
Margaret J. Wheatley

This chapter addresses the part in wellness played by a supportive community in your life. A supportive community may be a religious congregation, a group following a particular system or teacher, or a collection of likeminded friends. Supportive communities are within and across other communities.

Peaceful warriors aren't loners. They find the company of fellow seekers—friends on the path, spiritual friends. Our fellow seekers help us maintain confidence in our process; they are sources of knowledge. They lovingly "push our buttons" and confront us with our blind spots, and they provide the safety and loving acceptance we need to be well and happy.

## It Matters Whom We Hang Out With

Whom we spend our time with matters. Neuroscience and personal experience tell us we are like tuning forks; individual "vibrations," mood, and behavior are contagious.

As we know, as simple as it is, it is not easy to confront inner workings and cultivate new mental and physical habits. We need feedback and instruction from helpers—coaches, therapists, teachers, and peers. To borrow a line from the Beatles, "I get by with a little help from my friends."

The relationship with helpers like gurus, therapists, ministers, and coaches, is complex—a perfect place to practice relationship yoga. Beware of emotional attachment, clinging, hierarchies, and charlatans.

It has been my experience that communities that support open-minded inquiry and the goal of having its members come to know the guru within and weave a personal path are the best. Those that keep you bound to them may be temporarily useful but, in the end, they need to be honored and left behind. When you are ready you burn the boat. *(As a reminder to balance confidence in your understanding and capability, and the skillful doubt that questions everything, see the chapter on "Belief and Doubt.")*

## Social Intelligence

Community is the realm of social intelligence—interpersonal competencies built on specific neural circuits (and related endocrine systems) that inspire others to be effective.[56] Researchers have found that when people exhibit empathy and become attuned to others' moods, this action affects their own brain and the brain of others, as if their minds are part of a single system, as opposed to two or more brains reacting to one another.[57] Mirror neurons are the brain cells that contribute to empathy and to the way we feel when we are in the company of others. It is likely that this dynamic operates in any social interaction.

Our moods, our "vibe," affects our performance as individuals and groups. This is *emotional contagion*—the influence of your

---

[56] Goleman, Daniel, Boyartzis, Richard E., "Social Intelligence and the Biology of Leadership," *Harvard Business Review*, September 2008, https://hbr.org/2008/09/social-intelligence-and-the-biology-of-leadership
[57] Ibid.

emotional state on others, as if we were part of a unified nervous system.

Emotional contagion highlights the responsibility to cultivate positive qualities like empathy, kindness, appreciation, and open-hearted acceptance. Caught up in difficult emotions, you are less able to deal effectively with what is going on, and you transmit your fear, anger, or despair to those around you, making them fearful, angry, or sad.

In the chapter on "Love," there was mention of using a shield to protect the heart. We need the shield because sometimes the feelings we pick up from others can be overwhelming. For example, when you are in the company of someone who is angry, your shield (your mindfulness and emotional intelligence) helps you avoid being influenced by their emotion, reacting in fear or spiraling the anger.

But using the shield doesn't mean to hide from your feelings; it means to manage them to enhance wellness, your own and your community's. To use the shield wisely, apply self-awareness to experience the effect others are having on you, and self-management to act appropriately, along with the social awareness that lets you see what effect you are having on others.

## Friends on the Path

In addition to enabling us to increase social intelligence and experience calm and confidence, a supportive community offers friends on the path. "Friends on the path," or spiritual friends, help us stay focused on the commitment to wellness. They help us to avoid feeling as if we are alone and perhaps insane. They include teachers, coaches, and peers who are also working to free themselves of self-imposed stress.

In Herman Hesse's novel *Siddhartha*, the title character loses touch with his search for self-awareness when he has no connection to his spiritual friends and teachers. He becomes lost in the world of money, power, and sensuality. He says, "I had to spend many years like that to lose my intelligence, to lose the power to think, to forget about the unity of things."[58]

You need *spiritual* friends. It is important to have people in your life who share your motivation and understanding, and who are working to develop insight to overcome attachment, aversion, and ignorance. Without them you can feel as if you are a bit crazy, or you may become lulled to sleep because everyone around you is asleep.

But be careful of cults and groups that cut you off from general society and insist on blind belief. It may be useful to be in a closed, supportive community where you can more easily confront and overcome old conditioning and experience positive feelings of acceptance and caring. However, wellness relies on the ability to live in the world with its uncertainty, complexity, and change, and its diversity of people with varying degrees of awareness, knowledge, intelligence, and accomplishment.

Being isolated and protected in a closed community may feel right, and you might even be okay with being there for a time. But for most peaceful warriors, it is a stopover on the journey to wellness and a place to return periodically for refueling.

## Realigned Relationships

As you learn and practice cultivating wellness and dynamic balance, your lifestyle and relationships may change. Each change becomes another opportunity for self-awareness, acceptance, and letting go.

Everything changes. Relationships change as priorities, values, and views change. Some practitioners report that what was once entertaining has become boring. As tastes change, old friends may have less in common. Some people will choose to change jobs and

---

[58] Hermann Hesse, *Siddhartha*, Translated by Hilda Rosner, Bantam Books, July 1971, p. 96.

careers in order to seek wellness and balance. Primary relationships may change as partners change the way they think, feel, and respond. The groups or communities in which you once found yourself at home may become obstacles to your personal growth.

Changing relationships are yet another opportunity to practice acceptance, and skillfully let go into the experience with empathy, compassion, and lovingkindness.

## Finding Your Friends

There is no one way to find your community of friends on the path, and your teachers. It is often said that when the student is ready, the teaching will appear.

For me, it was an organic unfolding, starting with a neighborhood yoga class, and then some talks and retreats with recommended teachers that led me into a wide-ranging community of like-minded practitioners.

Start studying and practicing and you will find yourself meeting people with similar interests in classes, on social media, in local groups, churches, mosques, or synagogues, and even randomly striking up a conversation at a party. Somehow beginning to act on the intention to practice leads you on.

As said, be careful. Trust in your intuition, your ability to "read the vibes" of a group. Treat the search for community as if you are testing a hot tub. Put your toe in to see how it feels. Be patient. Watch the urge to join and the urge to stand apart—more fuel for working on yourself.

## EXERCISE
## Community of Friends on the Path

Reflect on the following questions and track your experience in community over the months and years you practice self-awareness, accepting, and letting go.

How well do the people in your life reinforce and strengthen your resolve to be happy and free of unnecessary stress?

How does it feel when you spend time with people who value and work to be self-aware, empathetic, compassionate, and kind?

How does it feel to be with "true believers" who are trying to convince you (and themselves) that *their* way is best for you?

CHAPTER 38

# The Bottom Line

*"In this hour Siddhartha ceased struggling with his fate, ceased suffering. On his face blossomed the serenity of knowledge, which no will opposes any longer, knowing perfection, in agreement with the flow of events, with the stream of life, full of compassion, full of sympathy, abandoned to the flow, belonging to unity."*
Hermann Hesse

The goal is wellness through self-awareness, accepting and letting go.

You have choice. You can experience, act, adjust, allow, and respond, to sustain dynamic balance as you use everything you encounter as an opportunity to live optimally. That is perfection, complete with pleasure and pain. Optimal living is a process of uncluttering, getting out of your own way, to experience the natural clarity and peace hidden behind the clutter—the beliefs, habits, likes and dislikes, and all the other stuff—that drives behavior.

The problem is unnecessary stress, resulting in anxiety, depression, anger, and other challenging emotions. These get in the way of effective, optimal living.

We face increasing volatility, complexity, and uncertainty as technology, AI, environmental change, diversity, organizational change, globalization, war, politics, and the blurring of the difference between truth, belief, theory, and fantasy converge with the realities of relationships, aging, sickness, and death. But while these factors may trigger stress, they do not cause the suffering. That cause is ignorance and clinging (attachment and aversion) to the desire for things to be different than they can be.

The solution is to accept what cannot be changed and let go into an active Flow that engages your intelligence, skills, and experience. Do the work to change the habits, beliefs, and biases that stand in your way by adopting realistic mental models and methods until you are ready to let go of even those—to burn the boat.

There is a passage in which Hesse's Siddhartha says to the Buddha, "Nobody will attain salvation by means of teachings." The concepts help but they do not reveal the "mystery" of being present, awake, and aware. The mystery is revealed when, on your own path, you go beyond concept to practice, using all life experience as fuel for the work of accepting and letting go.

If you don't want to explore the mystery, use the same methods and concepts to reduce stress and make yourself more effective and happier in whatever you do.

To live optimally, become a peaceful warrior:

- Accept and let go of habits, beliefs, and biases that get in the way of wellness.
- Patiently and persistently step back into a calm, peaceful center—the eye of the storm, the space behind the waterfall, or whatever you want to call it.
- Cultivate wellness by crafting and adopting a path that fits your life and uses every experience as fuel for your wellness journey.
- Go beyond concept using practices to experience things as they are.
- Remember, "All the world is a stage." Take your play both seriously and lightly.
- Become comfortable in the discomfort of free fall, uncertainty, and change to be cognitively ready—relaxed,

centered, confident, flexible, adaptable, resilient, grateful, forgiving, kind, and compassionate.
- Be kind and let waves of love, peace, and healing flow out through you in all directions.

*The path is the goal.*

# Glossary

The following glossary contains definitions of key words and phrases in the book, which were marked with an asterisk (*).

| Term | Definition |
|---|---|
| Ashram | In Hinduism, a place of spiritual retreat, separated from the rest of society and devoted to spiritual activities like yoga, meditation, or religious instruction. |
| Attachment | Clinging to what cannot be kept; needing things to be different than they can be. |
| Aversion | Clinging to the need to push away and deny what you feel is unpleasant. |
| Awake | Conscious, alert, attentive, and aware of yourself, impermanence, and your interdependence with all things. |
| Awareness | A non-conceptual knowing. Being aware. It is a subtle, ever-present quality of mind that we may be unaware of; awakening is the recognition of awareness. |
| Beautiful monsters | A term used by Tsoknyi Rinpoche for emotions, particularly the difficult ones |
| Calm abiding | The experience of simply resting comfortably in the present moment. See *serenity, calm center, equanimity*. |

# GLOSSARY

| Term | Definition |
|---|---|
| Calm center | The calm center is not really a center. It is a state of equilibrium, the felt sense of a point that opens into awareness, the platform from which you act most effectively. It is home, a place of comfort, and refuge.<br><br>In touch with calm, clarity, and a sense of serenity, peace, and comfort, whether you are in motion or at rest. |
| Clinging | Clinging is holding on, needing things to be different than they can be. It is a principal cause of suffering. |
| Compassion | The heartfelt desire to avoid or alleviate suffering. Feeling what others feel as if you were feeling it; seeing them as no different than you. |
| Dukkha | A Pali and Sanskrit term that means sorrow or suffering. In Buddhist thought it is caused by attachment, aversion, and ignorance. |
| Dynamic balance | Dynamic balance is stability while in motion, flexible, adapting to the moment. It is the experience of *Flow*—fluid performance as if no one were performing. It is like walking a tightrope. It is to be in a calm center when everything is in motion in an interdependent process. |
| Ego | Refers to the sense of self that is created by the continuous appearance of thoughts, feelings, physical sensations, and concepts driven by our thoughts, experiences, and conditioning. |

# GLOSSARY

| Term | Definition |
|---|---|
| Emotion | A feeling, a felt sense, a mental state different from reason or knowledge, a reaction to circumstances, conditioning, mood, and relationships. Emotional reactions release chemicals in the brain which are experienced as strong physical feelings usually towards a specific person, event, or object. |
| Enlightenment | Freedom from ignorance, attachment, and aversion. |
| Equanimity | A sense of calm in the face of anything. It is to be in touch with a *calm center*. Being equanimous: calm and composed. |
| Expectation | A strong belief or hope that something will happen. |
| Felt sense | A deep feeling. The wordless, thought-free, direct experience of what we are feeling. It is related to gut instinct and to proprioception (the ability to sense movement, action, and location). It is what scientists call enteroception, the sense of the internal state of the body that is important for maintaining balance and enabling self-awareness. |
| Flow | Being fully engaged, effortlessly performing as best as possible, and at the same time observing it all without thinking about it or interfering with the performance. It is as if the action was happening without an actor. It is synonymous with being "in the Zone." |

# GLOSSARY

| Term | Definition |
|---|---|
| Ignorance | Not accepting the reality of interdependence, inevitable change, uncertainty, a false sense of self, and that things will not always go as you'd like them to. Also called delusion. The opposite of being awake and aware. |
| Kindness | Wishing that oneself and others are well—happy, healthy, prosperous, free of unnecessary suffering. Acting in a friendly, generous, considerate way. |
| Mantra | Sound or phrase that may be chanted out loud or silently. The word is from Sanskrit: *Man* means to think and *tra* to liberate. Mantra is a thought or sound that liberates or clears the mind. |
| Meditation | Meditation is a mental exercise to achieve wellness by cultivating concentration, mindfulness, and calm abiding. |
| Mindfulness | A natural quality of mind that objectively observes without thinking about observing or about what is being observed. |
| Mindset | The attitudes, perceptions, beliefs, and mental models that determine behavior and emotional responses. |
| Model | A representation of something (for example, ideas, processes) and how it operates. A worldview is a model of how the world works. |
| Namaste | Traditional Hindu greeting<br><br>A deeper meaning is, *I greet that which is in you that is also in me.* It is an acknowledgement that in our hearts we are one, we are interdependent, and we all may be driven by mental habits, biases, and neuroses. |

# GLOSSARY

| Term | Definition |
|---|---|
| Neuroplasticity | The brain's ability to form and reorganize the pathways that influence feelings, thinking, and behavior. |
| Neuroscience | The study of how the nervous system works focusing on the brain and the way it influences behavior and cognition. |
| Neuroses | Mental conditions involving out-of-proportion emotional stress characterized by anxiety, depression, anger, and other feelings of unhappiness and distress. |
| Non-dual thinking (non-duality) | The idea that there is an indescribable boundless whole within which life's movie is unfolding. Everything is appearing and dissolving in boundless space, as images appear in a mirror. |
| Peaceful warrior | One dedicated to personal freedom and expanded self-awareness with the intention to improve one's own wellness and to improve the wellness of those around us. A courageous explorer. |
| Process | A set of steps that creates an outcome, a result like a fresh coat of paint, a decision, or an emotional reaction. Process thinking says that every outcome is the result of a process. |
| Reality | Things as they are—impermanent, uncertain, sometimes painful, out of your complete control. The totality of events, entities, and states. |

# GLOSSARY

| Term | Definition |
|---|---|
| Self-awareness | Self-awareness is knowing who or what we are, our goals and intentions, strengths, and weaknesses, and the way the mind works, our inner workings. It is realizing that the blend of these affects our behavior. Self-awareness is the foundation for emotional and social intelligence. It enables self-management, the ability to choose how to respond rather than to react.<br><br>There is no single accepted definition; see the section *"Self-Awareness: Who Are You?"* |
| Serenity | A state of being composed, calm, patient, peaceful, and untroubled. Another word for equanimity. |
| System | A set of things (principles, processes, procedures, people, organizations, etc.) working together as part of a whole. |
| System Thinking | A way of looking at the universe as a system of intersecting systems within systems. |
| The Zone | Being in Flow. |
| Transpersonal | Beyond the limits of personality or ego identity |
| Wellness | Being healthy in the sense of a dynamically balanced lifestyle to sustain optimal physical, mental, emotional, intellectual, social, occupational, financial, and environmental health. |
| Wisdom | Deep understanding, a felt sense of the way things are and the intention to skillfully apply that understanding in life. Wisdom is the antidote to ignorance that cuts the roots of clinging and is displayed as compassion. |

# GLOSSARY

| Term | Definition |
|---|---|
| Worldview | A model of how the universe works, where we fit in it, the way our inner and outer processes and beliefs affect us and our relationships, and how we can affect them. |
| Yoga | A system of spiritual self-development for training the mind through bodywork, self-observation, awareness and letting go. Yoga means "union" or "oneness." |

# About the Author

Many years ago, I made the commitment to use my life experience as the fuel for a gradual unfolding of the ability to be happy even when sad, mad, or scared. It is an ongoing process.

I have practiced meditation and yoga for 50 years, 30 years as a meditation teacher and coach, with decades of wide-ranging experience in the world of organizations, technology, teams, family, and community, in roles as a C-level technology executive, speaker, author, coach, software developer, project management expert, spouse, father, grandfather, uncle, and friend.

My mindset and worldview are influenced by systems and process thinking, non-dual meditation, and devotional practices. I have learned from world-class teachers of yoga, mindfulness, Tai Chi Chuan, non-duality, leadership, and Eastern and Western psychology.

My greatest struggles have been with anger and impatience. My greatest influencers have been the practice of *kundalini* and *hatha* yoga, the devotional teachings of Ram Dass and Neem Karoli Baba, and non-dual teachings from Advaita and Tibetan Buddhist Dzogchen teachers.

All that to discover that all there is to live as best as possible is to accept, learn from experience, and let go of anything that impedes being present, loving, and in Flow.

## ABOUT THE AUTHOR

After decades, there are still many opportunities to accept, learn, and let go, though there are increasingly frequent and longer-lasting moments of being awake, present, and content with the movement of things as they are. And I am in less of a rush to be "enlightened," knowing that the journey itself is the destination.

I offer the expression of my experience as a service to inform others for their unique journeys.

*George Pitagorsky*